Talking with Nature

Talking
with Nature

*Sharing the Energies and Spirit of
Trees, Plants, Birds, and Earth*

BY MICHAEL J. ROADS

H J Kramer Inc
Tiburon, California

Published by H J Kramer Inc
P.O. Box 1082, Tiburon, CA 94920

ISBN 0-915811-06-5

Cover art: Genevieve Wilson
Cover design: Abigail Johnston
Production: Kimberly Freeman
Interior illustration: Genevieve Wilson

Originally published in Australia as
Communicating With Nature
(ISBN 0-9590152-4-8)
by Night Owl Publishers Pty Ltd

Revised United States edition, 1987

Manufactured in the United States of America

10   9   8   7   6   5   4   3   2   1

To my darling Treenie, with love.
The Fairy Ring is growing!

Contents

Foreword

THIS IS A LOVELY, extraordinary book. For many, it will open the way to a new connection with Nature.

Nature is a great work of art and design, a fantastic, intricate, ever-flowing Oneness, of which we are an integral part. We of the civilized world now feel separate from Nature because in the last centuries we have become onlookers and seek only to control Nature for power and profit. We, the rightful stewards of the planet, have failed lamentably and culpably in our stewardship and are rapidly turning this beautiful world into a desert.

In the past centuries, the sensitive feminine faculties of the right hemisphere of the brain have largely gone dormant and become atrophied. These poetical and imaginative powers can apprehend the Living Whole. We must now renew our awareness that visible Nature is the form; the heart is the living Idea. The human being, that crown of evolution, has been so designed that he or she can blend in thought with these Ideas.

Realize the great truth that each of us is a droplet of divinity, a spiritual being housed in a temple, the body, which enables us to operate in the heavy density of the material world. We have become so imbued with the "onlooker consciousness" that we too easily assume that God or our guides will speak to us from outside. But the great truth is that the beings of the higher worlds speak to us *within our own thinking.* All is Thought; in thinking we blend with higher beings.

God speaks to us within our thinking. God is within every flower and tree, animal and bird, crystal and cloud and ocean wave. Therefore, it follows that humanity, once over the barrier of conceptual separation, can blend and unite *in thinking* with the higher worlds.

Now we are offered this remarkable book describing one man's experience. If the author can achieve this "talking with nature" then all of us can potentially do the same. The manner of approach and attitude of mind are what matter. Approach the natural form—tree or hill, river or blossom—and speak inwardly with the elemental being within it. Then watch the response in your mind and heart and give back love. Let the flow begin. This form of meditation is awakening the "eye of the mind."

This book is a beautiful statement of this experience, which is open to us all. Those who achieve it are part of the awakening of Planet Earth, for humanity now stands at the threshold of a birth into wider consciousness of the great Oneness of all life.

Of course, this is the knowledge of the mystics and initiates of all ages. It has in our time been well demonstrated in such centers as Findhorn in Scotland, where Peter Caddy, through his sensitive friend Dorothy Maclean, established direct telepathic contact with elemental beings. The result was a fabulous garden of vegetables, fruits, and flowers grown in arid sand dunes. The desert can indeed blossom like the rose when man contacts and works with the nature spirits and devas.

This, Michael Roads's experience and achievement, is a wonderful step and an inspiring example. Read this book and learn how each of us can make this approach. It is an aspect of the great awakening of humanity now taking place on the threshold of the Aquarian Age.

Sir George Trevelyan
Badminton, Avon
May 15, 1987

Publisher's Preface

Talking with Nature is a book that cries out for special attention. It is the story of a man who discovered he possessed the ability to commune intelligently and articulately with the souls of plants, animals, and even rocks and rivers. It evokes the same sense of contact with the miraculous that distinguished Carlos Castaneda's early work.

At first, Michael Roads found himself disturbed by his strange new power. He questioned it relentlessly. Finally, when he could no longer deny his experience, he allowed Nature to nourish and heal him. Nature spoke to him of her deep concern with the role of man in determining the fate of the Earth. With patience, compassion, and even humor, she taught him how to become one with the whole of creation.

Talking with Nature is an important book because it offers a new way for those who want to heal the wounds of alienation and become reunited in loving awareness with the natural world.

The message of the book is one of hope for us all. A solution is in sight. Like Michael Roads, all mankind can learn to accept and listen to the voices of Nature. We can learn to reconnect ourselves with the spiritual essence of the universe.

Michael Roads has taken a giant step. The nourishment of the soul, body, and spirit which Nature offered to him is available to us all. He speaks to us of the gift of joyful reconciliation. Nature can be our friend instead of our adversary. She can instruct us in finding our way back to the true path. The birds, plants, rivers, winds are praying for us. Will we listen to them before it is too late? Can we learn to hear in time?

I believe we can. That is why I publish this book with such special enthusiasm.

Harold Kramer, Publisher

Acknowledgments

First and foremost, I wish to thank Treenie for "believing" in me. Without her support and encouragement this book would never have been written. Togetherness is the key which helped unlock the hidden.

To Richard Bach, who has proved that words can bridge time and distance, I offer my special thanks for the comment on the cover and for his loving support and inspiration.

To Hal Kramer, a publisher who not only believes in changing lives, but actually makes it happen, my deepest gratitude.

My thanks to the universe for sending Linda Tellington-Jones to visit with such perfect timing.

Thanks also to my editor, Greg Armstrong, who edited my manuscript with great sensitivity and caring.

Every writer needs to be discovered by a person sensitive to their potential. My special thanks to Linda Lutzkendorf who recognized the potential of this book and helped to make it possible.

Jack Igguldon, who was my first literary critic, advisor, and mentor—thank you.

Various people throughout my life have been important catalysts. With perfect timing they have revealed my life's path, and always in accordance with my faltering stumble. To these people, whom I count as very special friends, thank you.

Talking with Nature

1
September

THE PLATYPUS DISAPPEARED UNDERWATER as though sucked downward, so effortless was its passing. Not far away, wind whistled through the long, thin needles of a solitary River Oak, a high melody of sound invoking a feeling of coolness despite the warmth of the spring sun. A slight breeze moved the leaves near where I was sitting on the river bank. The water flowed cool and clear, sparkling in the sun from endless flickering points of light.

"Help me," I asked.

I spoke to the river, to the rocks, to all the different plants which grew in a semitropical profusion around me. I spoke to Nature. Inside, I felt it was smiling at me.

Help yourself. If you wish to tell the story of our connection, then write from the point of contact which you are.

This was not going to be easy. I tried again.

"What I need is help to explain in a concise and simple way the human connection with Nature. I need something that people can relate to. Something which is easy to understand and accept."

The smile became more pronounced.

You are suggesting some written material which does not stretch the imagination, something simple enough for the mind to comprehend.

"That's it," I said triumphantly. "Just the thing."
The smile vanished.

Forget it. How can we write of unseen realities, hint of unheard concepts, or even demonstrate the practicality of inner truths, without disturbing the slumbering Self within?

A long, deep sigh.

We have a choice, my friend. Either you write it as it happens, as it is revealed, or forget the whole project. I can offer no compromise. Accept it. This will be written as a synthesis of man and Nature.

For a long time I stared across the river, trying to pretend it was not happening this way. Surely I could write my book the way I wanted. It was mine to control. The rock beneath me was very patient. In a physical sense it had not moved in a very long time, but I could feel a surge of conscious activity. I was plagued with a cross-section of thoughts. Who will believe me if I present it the way it is happening? Surely the best plan is to disguise the issue and make a story of it? The thought of *Jonathan Livingston Seagull* crossed my mind. Problem is, that's already been done. This is ridiculous. I cannot just write that I listen to trees and rocks and rivers, that I talk to them and they talk back into my mind. I squirmed and fidgeted, pretending I could not hear the river chuckling as it flowed smoothly past my rock.

I could feel an expectancy around me. The trees all looked their normal, majestic, indifferent selves, while the rocks maintained a solid silence. A Heron swooped down, bright eyed and alert. Deciding I was no threat, it carefully alighted on the gravel on the opposite side of the river and, cocking its head to one side, held me with a fixed stare.

"Okay," I said. "If you have an opinion we might as well hear it."

There was a powerful feeling of bird energy moving into the more subtle areas of awareness.

We would also like to be involved. If you are going to write of our connection, then we will represent our own point of view.

I stared at the Heron.

"Do you represent all birds or just your own species?"

The Heron stabbed into the shallows, its rapier beak flashing downward in an action defying the eye. Thrusting itself into the air, it winged slowly away.

We represent ourselves only. We will contact you when the time is right.

The consciousness of Heron was curling in upon itself, becoming smaller and fading swiftly. It was interesting to realize that in no way was it a single, solitary bird which spoke into my mind. Rather the bird was no more than a trigger for my slowly developing awareness. It was the point of focus which allowed me to be aware that the Heron consciousness waited for me, not wishing to impose on my mind unannounced. I stared at the words I had written.

"Nobody's going to believe this."

I spoke to the river flowing past my feet. For a while there was silence. I became aware of a surge of power from the river as though there was a gathering of force.

You have already reached your decision. It was made long before you came here. I suggest you now allow the clarity of a higher truth to move through you. The fear you have established is a real one and it can cause problems. You will now need to act in trust, knowing that the timing is right. Only the few will mock you. Those who are attracted to this book will have an inner hunger which seeks appeasement.

Your words will not be easy to digest. Questions will be asked and much inner dialogue will be worked through. This, however, is not your concern.

A favorite quotation by Victor Hugo moved swiftly across my mind: "Nothing has greater power than an idea whose time has arrived." It was a flash of illumination. The time "has" arrived. More and more people are looking for a higher truth and meaning in life, and what better starting place than our connection with Nature?

I smiled into the water.

"Okay, I'll do it your way, but if I am trying to present something which seems incredible, please help it to become credible."

The energy of river, coiled in an almost serpentine formlessness around me, was suddenly in motion. I had the fleeting sense of being in the center of a vast whirlpool, expanding outward with an exultant joy.

Go now. With acceptance comes expansion. If you can capture the experience on paper, this will be our mutual presentation to the people with whom you seek to communicate.

SEVERAL DAYS ELAPSED while I digested the first encounter and prepared to commit myself to paper. I read and reread my words.

Nobody was going to believe this.

Gradually I was forced to accept that it was I who found it most difficult to believe. I realized that I had yet to conquer my fears.

Just as Nature was my challenge, it was also my guide, so one sunny morning I returned to my favorite place by the river.

It was cold, but crystal clear. A yard below the water surface, a shoal of tiny fish faced into the current, floating effortlessly in their fluid environment. On the smooth stones beneath them, a large, solitary shrimp made its way slowly and carefully to an unknown destination, its antennae waving methodically around it. A catfish drifted slowly past, vanishing beneath an overhanging rock.

It was a tranquil scene, and I felt encouraged by the sense of peace around me. I greeted the river. "Well, I'm back and I'm keen to continue the book."

A feeling of coiled power was once more present.

Oh, it's THE book now, is it? Quite an improvement on your previous MY book. If you can retain such an unattached attitude we should have little difficulty.

I felt rather put down.

"You seem to imply that I'm the only one who could be wrong, or is likely to be difficult."

I paused, hoping for some verbal comfort.

While you sit comfortably wrapped in a pitying ego, we have nothing, nothing at all.

For the next ten minutes I gazed in hurt silence across the river. My feeling of resentment slowly faded as I watched the antics of an Eastern Water Dragon trying hard to reach a succulent insect at the end of a long, very thin branch overhanging the water. I could see a connection between the dragon's laborious efforts to reach the end of the branch and acquire his prize, and my own efforts to approach communication with Nature from a clear, uncluttered mind. The dragon was not equipped for stealth on a long, bending, waving branch, but on a riverside tree stump or rock it could be patience itself, leaping like an uncoiled spring when it was sure of its prey. The branch denied this, so it had to change style. A plop as the dragon dropped into the water indicated its lack of success. Swimming with head held high, the dragon disappeared under the branches of an overhanging shrub. I also was out on a limb. This limb was of my own making, supported by my old belief system, and sustained by my self-image to the world.

Words moved from the source of power.

Do as the dragon did. Let go and fall into the river. Let the river of life sweep you beyond all aid from old and worn con-

*cepts. I will support you. Trust me. As you swim from an old
consciousness, blind to higher realities beyond your physical
world, trust that I will guide you with care and love into a new
stream of consciousness. I will open a new world before you.
Can you trust me enough to let go of the known, and swim in
an unknown current?*

Even as I stared into the river, a dark cloud moved across
the sun. The water was no longer clear. Suddenly it was dark and
opaque, clouded with mystery and, to my reasoning mind,
loaded with threat. I knew this was the way it must be. If the
way before me was an old familiar scene, then I traveled the
known path.

"I accept. I will cast myself as fully as I can into the stream
you offer, and I am grateful. I ask only that you are patient with
me, for I have many old fears, and like the dragon, I cling from
long habit."

The cloud swept away and the river was again clear, sparkling with invitation. The power surged, slowly uncoiling with
an inner sigh. I felt a sense of peace and joy sweep over me.

My commitment was made.

M Y COMMITMENT TO THE TASK hadn't happened all at
once. It had unfolded like fate over the years during
my life as a farmer. I can look back now and recognize
the stages.

It began with my wife, Treenie.

One evening, while sitting relaxed in our living room, she
glanced at me. "The cows want moving," she suddenly
announced.

I snorted with indignation. Her statement seemed a challenge, and I responded.

"Right! Just to prove you're wrong, we'll drive up there
tomorrow at nine o'clock, and you can see for yourself all the
contented cows on plenty of pasture."

In my smug satisfaction, I burrowed back into my book.

Next morning at nine o'clock, Treenie and I drove up to the back paddock. Shock! Practically the entire herd of cows was standing impatiently at the gate, waiting to be let out. I gaped at them, not willing to meet Treenie's eyes. You can imagine her next comment!

them, not willing to meet Treenie's eyes. You can imagine her next comment!

This was not to be an isolated incident. Over the next few months Treenie often became aware of the herd's need to change paddocks, regardless of the amount of pasture available. It occurred to me that since Treenie could receive their "move" messages, we could influence them with our thoughts. One evening we combined our thoughts to reach them. *We will move you cattle at nine o'clock tomorrow morning.* Smile if you like, but next morning at nine o'clock the cattle were all waiting to be moved. Now, I am not suggesting cattle can tell the time, because we eventually proved that they would begin to congregate well before the chosen hour; but the method worked, consistently, showing a stunning disregard for logic or reason.

During this time an area of land we had bought from the Forestry Commission had been cleared, developed, and sown down to improved pasture. This land, known as Carvilla, lay at a 2,000-foot altitude, offering splendid views of the ocean along the north coast in one direction, while towering, rugged mountains dominated the other. Apart from where Carvilla joined our main farm at one end, the pasture was completely surrounded by unfenced forest, stretching as far as the eye could see over thousands of wild acres. Carvilla jutted as an elongated spur into the forest, possessing a long boundary. Not unnaturally, the wildlife were partial to a nibble of improved pasture and were lured in considerable numbers to our land.

With the organic development and improvement of the soil, Carvilla did not respond with growth the way I anticipated. I slowly realized that the forest wildlife was extracting a heavy toll from the new pasture.

After a few night visits, to my consternation, I found large numbers of Bennett's Wallaby (quite big fellows) and Scrub Wallabies and Pademelons in profusion. In the only way I knew to defend my pasture, I began to spend two nights a week shooting them. I quickly found it extremely distasteful, and rather than continue such a heartless task I contacted a few locals, offering them the opportunity to shoot for sport and meat—an offer quickly accepted. It seemed, however, to make little difference. The pasture which was carrying only thirty cows and calves made little extra growth.

To tip the balance in my favor, I decided I would have to become involved again; so once more I began night shooting. One night, after spotting a large wallaby in the headlights, I jumped out, rifle ready. The wallaby was only a few yards away as I raised my rifle. Suddenly the animal's head swung toward me, the shaft of light catching its eyes. Transformed to glowing red jewels, the eyes met mine, and I gazed spellbound into the soul of a wild and wonderful Nature. For long moments our eyes held, locked. Slowly and calmly the animal looked away and quietly grazed the pasture.

I stood silent, shocked to the core. Compassion, a comparative stranger to farmers saturated in death, surged powerfully from somewhere deep inside. I lowered my rifle and turned to walk back to the Landrover. There had to be a different way. Violence could not be the answer. Violence begets violence. I knew I could not reach my objective in this manner.

I had twice used 10–80 poison, but this was no solution. It is a shocking form of subtle violence, insidious by the absence of the poisoner to witness the agony of death. By its very involvement, a rifle at least places you in a position where you witness your action, demanding a clean kill as a code of ethics.

I talked the problem over with Treenie, and together we reached the only solution possible. If we could "think"-communicate with our cattle, why not try and "think"-communicate with the wallabies.

Making such a decision was one thing, but carrying it out was another. We decided I should be the one to initiate the move owing to my current involvement, but how should I instigate such a thing? One morning, driving up to the wild hills of Carvilla, I stopped near a group of trees in the center of the paddock and, feeling rather self-conscious, prepared myself for an attempted communication.

I held the required agreement clearly in my thoughts, but so silent and remote was the act that I began to verbalize my request. Despite feeling foolish, I felt more positive and comfortable. Warming to my task, I fairly yelled my message to all the wallabies that might listen. It sounded something like this:

"I don't know if you wallabies can hear me, but I am offering an agreement with you by which we each meet our own needs. I am asking you to stop eating our pasture, and in exchange for this I will see to it that nobody shoots you again. However, because I realize I must share this land with you, I will allow you to graze around the outside of the paddock. Please don't take more than twenty yards."

Following this announcement, I paused expectantly. Nothing! Nothing except the mental echo of my own words. I was in no way convinced that anything would happen, but to keep my side of the agreement I chained and padlocked the entrance gate and told the shooters that I wanted no more shooting on my land. Eyeing me as though I were nutty, they agreed. I felt glad I did not tell them the reason!

Within only a few weeks, the pasture was thickening so rapidly that I was able to introduce an extra ten cows and calves. It continued to improve. Soon I had ninety cows and calves grazing over Carvilla, while the white clover grew in abundance. For three years we maintained this tenuous agreement, the pastures continuing to thrive and flourish. When the pasture was knee-high it was crisscrossed with wallaby trails, but their grazing was concentrated at the boundary. I confess, whoever they chose to measure the twenty yards took mighty strides . . . or bounds! In some areas, pasture grew right to the forest edge, while in other places they fed a long way into the paddock. On average I estimated they grazed about forty yards into the field.

One fact which emerged was obvious. We were able to

communicate our wishes to the wildlife and reach an agreement for our mutual benefit. We recognized their divine right to life, realizing that cooperation with Nature offers unlimited potential.

There is a follow-up to this story. When we eventually decided to sell our farm, we sold it under separate titles. When the new occupants moved into Highfields, we retained ownership of Carvilla for another two years before selling it to the original buyer. During this time shooters broke the padlocks and, without our knowing, began shooting wallabies once more. When I visited the area three years after selling the farm, the owner asked me if pasture had ever grown on Carvilla. I stared at him in surprise.

"When I last walked Carvilla, white clover was knee-high," I said. He looked dour.

"Well, mate, I can assure you there's none there now," he replied.

He went on to tell me how he had found the place crawling with wallabies. They shot six thousand wallabies in two years! I was stunned. I realized immediately that such a number could not have been bred in such a short time. Considering the huge amount of forest, I had suspected there were large numbers in the area when we made our agreement, but I had no idea I was dealing with such numbers. It was only then I fully understood the extent to which our agreement had been kept. Apparently, as soon as the shooting began, the wallabies swarmed in, and, despite six thousand shot, they literally wiped out the pasture. I felt shocked, guilty, and angry. But what could I say? I had never told him about the agreement — who would believe such a thing?

WE HAD BEEN MILKING for about eight years when dairying slid into economic decline. It was the perfect moment to merge the Friesian dairy herd into the Friesian/Hereford herd we had been breeding for several years and turn to beef farming.

One happy morning, I began the long-awaited task of demolishing the despised milking yards. It was blissful, but it proved to be a much tougher job than I anticipated. The rails were solidly welded water pipes. Swinging a fourteen-pound sledgehammer, I attacked each joint with eight years of pent-up ferocity, and it did not take long to raise some large blisters on my already-calloused hands. By using around twenty blows per joint, the yard slowly and painfully succumbed. Halfway through I was wiped out. As I sat quietly resting, a change of attitude moved through me, precipitated by an incredible thought. *If all life is connected, then the animal, mineral, and vegetable kingdoms are interconnected. Knowing the coopera-tion I have experienced with plants and animals, why should metal be so different?*

Gradually I surrendered to an inner peace, feeling some oh-so-subtle shift take place within. Refreshed, I stood up and, grasp-ing the sledgehammer, prepared for another onslaught! Subtly, so subtly, the words moved easily into my mind.

Change your attitude. See the metal as living. Respect the material, the form of life. Approach the task with humility.

It all fit. I felt comfortable with this odd thought, even if I had no more than a surface understanding. I swung the sledgehammer with little force, my mind on the metal, once — twice — the third blow, and the end of the rail fell away. Rapidly I moved to the other end and repeated it. Two hours later, the yard was dismantled. Only then did I feel stunned . . . and frustrated. I mean, who would ever believe such a thing?

WE REACHED A STAGE where we were committed to sell-ing the farm. We had several reasons. I had a chronic back injury, and we were fed up with the financial pressure. But, above and beyond all the normal, mundane rea-sons, something else beckoned. I cannot give it a name, or easily identify it, but within Nature I had become aware of another dimension. A dimension which, when explored, promised to vastly enrich our lives. A different truth was calling to us, for we were no longer the same people who had commenced farming a decade earlier in Australia.

I had become deeply involved with the organic farming movement in Tasmania. When Treenie and I were workers at a weekend Organic Field Demonstration, I was introduced to a tall, bearded American with a Florida drawl. Hunter Lilly, a man in his late twenties, strolled into our lives as though he were a long-lost wayward son. It seemed natural that he would return home with us, becoming part of the family until we left Tasmania. The farm was sold and we were in the last few weeks of selling stock, tidying our affairs, farewelling friends, and attending to all the numerous things that need attention when a family of six decide to go nomadic for a lengthy period. The situation was practically under control when Hunter suggested he and I walk the South Coast Track. The reference did not mean much to me, but when he pointed it out on a map, I realized it was a walk of approximately 110 miles, with a small proportion on the remote, isolated, south coast beaches.

After some misgivings I agreed to accompany him. We made our preparations, and Treenie drove us on the six-hour journey down to Cockles Creek, south of Hobart. As she drove away, leaving us to face the wilderness, my misgivings once again bubbled to the surface. The night before we left home I had a very powerful dream. I dreamed that I had died. The dream was not frightening, but the experience was unusually strong. I stood with an angel in a cathedral-like valley, surrounded by people who were close and dear to me. I was overwhelmed. I knew these people, yet I didn't know them! But I knew, clearly, that I was dead. Anyway, I had been walking only an hour when the first blister emerged on one heel, and the ill-fitting, sixty-pound pack began to make its presence known. I wondered then if I might die on this walk, so powerful was the dream experience.

By the end of the first day of the ten-day walk, I had developed blisters on the heels of both feet. I had learned too late of the need for proper, thorough preparation for serious bush walks in a kind of wilderness from which some unfortunate people never emerge.

We walked—correction, Hunter walked, I limped—day after day through some of the world's most rugged and beautiful country. After eight days' walking filled with adventure and danger, some grim moments and some hilarious ones, we decided to rest for three days in a bush-walker's hut at Melaleuca, a remote, lonely tin-miner's retreat, miles from anywhere. There I attempted to heal my wounded heels. The blisters had long since turned into holes gouged into the flesh, which bled freely as I walked.

The attempt was futile. When we set off on our last two days of walking, it took only an hour for the wounds to reopen. I continued to our destination, Lake Pedder, in a blur of pain. Tormented shoulders met and merged with the pain lancing up from ravaged heels.

We started off on our last day at seven o'clock in the morning, determined that it would indeed be the last day. It was about four o'clock in the afternoon, and walking at the pace we had set had become an automatic process. We were already long overdue, and I knew Treenie would be getting really worried. We had walked hard for nine hours on the last day, and by four o'clock I had reached a stage where my fatigue was so dominant that toes squishing in my own blood were no longer important. I had become a walking-machine, lost in a blur of pain. We were heavily laden because of the extreme weather conditions—especially the wind which swept the southern land mass of this area, which is not terribly far from the Antarctic. Within my pain I was completely isolated from any outer reality. My environment had shrunk to one of pain—walk—pain—walk—keep on keeping on. We had at least three hours' walking ahead of us, and we were now not only racing time, but also a colossal storm which had been building up all day. Repeatedly I told myself I would collapse after the next fifty paces—another fifty—pain and walk. My mind was dazed, my body numb as I thought, "God, I can't

keep going. What do I do?" Without doubt my exhaustion erased
all resistance, for into my mind, powerfully, came a flow
of words.

*Why do you choose to walk this way, alone and alienated
from the surrounding abundance of energy? The plants around
you are filled with energy; all life is energy. This is yours if only
you can be aware that you are not separate; you are part of a
Whole. Be open, be loving. Become All in One, the One in All.*

Exhaustion erased resistance. I do not know how, but in a
blaze of inner realization came "knowing," and with this
"knowing" came energy. In moments I was a powerhouse —
vital, alive, and aware — while the pain receded to no more than
a background murmur, unimportant in the overall act of life. I
became "one" with my environment. Suddenly I was alive in a
way never before experienced. I related to every twig, every leaf,
each blade of grass, the living soil, the fading, watery sun. All
became part of myself, and I in turn became part of the Whole.
Hunter, who was leading the way, was also nearly out on his feet,
and, as I watched him stumbling along, I felt such a love for him
— for all he was as a person — that my "knowing" also encompassed him. I called out, "Hunter. Let love embrace you in its
power. Love, Hunter. Love your environment." As I had been, he
was too exhausted to question my sanity, or resist my words, and
the same energy which had entered me swept him up also, our
pace doubling and trebling as we strode along. Two hours later
when we sat in the only other shelter of the walk, with the
storm raging around us, Hunter looked at me, paused, and with
awe in his voice asked, "Wow, what happened back there?"

What indeed?

It was as though the incredible culmination of this journey
highlighted a series of connections with Nature dating back to
my childhood. With this experience fresh in my mind, all previous experiences fused into "one," standing on the edge of some
other, unknown dimension, and offering a journey into states of
consciousness requiring courage . . . and surrender. I needed to

surrender fear, fear of the unknown. For, strangely, the deeper this inner journey went, the stronger grew a mysterious, inexplicable fear.

One night I had a dream of such clarity and depth, of such color and feeling that it is forever imprinted in my memory. In my dream it was late evening on a sultry night. High in the sky a full moon lit up the beach on which I was standing, while each gentle wave reflected a million rippling stars. The sand was white, reflecting and highlighting the pearly moon glow; the sea murmured quietly as it caressed the beach. I stood alone, my head back, gazing at the stars. I was not surprised when a falling star streaked across the sky, seeming to land almost on the beach before it flickered out. A few minutes passed, and giving a deep, contented sigh I began to walk away from the sea toward a distant cottage — my home.

Only then did I notice a figure walking toward me from the direction of the falling star. Somehow I knew this person was looking for me, so I stopped, waiting quietly. As the figure approached, I realized it was a man, his face shadowed. He was only yards from me when the moonlight caught his face, illuminating his features.

I gazed at myself! Shock numbed and paralyzed me. I could only raise my arms, feebly trying to hold this other me away, but with a smile he/I walked right into me — and we merged.

Instantly, everything changed! The way I had experienced the whole world ceased — and a new reality emerged. I "knew" deeply and intimately every grain of sand on the beach. Each grain was as individual as you and I. Each had an identity. Each had a sound. I listened to a celestial sound which is quite indescribable. Cosmic song, music of the spheres, song of the universe — none can describe that sound of immeasurable richness. Sound which I could not only hear, but also feel and see. Sound which I became, for only in becoming could it be experienced. Each molecule of water in the ocean became "known." No other words can describe it. I "knew." Every star in the sky became "known."

Closer than a loved one in normal life, I was as close to the universe as life itself. I was whole, complete, vibrant—the All in All—the One in All—the All in One. I watched colors which have neither name nor meaning swirling and merging all around me. Color and sound, visual and auditory, became "One" within me.

How long this all lasted I do not know, but there came a moment when this other I stepped away from me and walked slowly away. The effect was devastating. To say I felt as though I was cast into the densest, blackest hole in existence, blind, deaf, dumb, and drugged beyond feeling, would not be an exaggeration. Desperately I called out to the departing me, "Please . . . help me . . . don't leave me like this."

The figure turned around, pity on his/my face, walked toward me and embraced me. Normality returned, my normal world . . . and I woke up.

I lay for a while, shocked and distressed. It had ended, but I had not been asleep. I knew I had experienced a peak reality. I was not awakening from a dream, I was falling asleep after experiencing heightened awareness.

My dull and cluttered normal senses defied an intimate relationship with Nature. I could not deny the experience by saying, "Just a dream." Inside my heart I was aware I had been involved in life's movement in a way denied to normal physical reality. I was deeply grateful, yet I suffered an overwhelming sense of loss. The song was no more. Not a song of a physical world, but of the realms of Spirit. It was a song of life, of promise.

The tiny flame which had ignited in me during the times of isolation as a youth was renewed, revived; yet at the same time, a vague fear which haunted the back of my mind, moving as a ghost through ancient memories, was also fanned into life.

Simultaneously there moved into my life a deep inner conviction of the dream being a reality I wanted to consciously experience and a fear which was to try every conceivable way to make me undermine such a conviction. This fear carried the power of a death threat. I could not understand it, yet it was an energy which was to put me through years of self-doubt and mental anguish.

V ERY EARLY ONE MORNING a friend and I were driving at a steady eighty miles per hour in his rather beat-up panel van, when in front of us a huge Old Man Kangaroo moved his mob off the road, bounding into the scrub with deceptive ease. A fawn-colored doe paused after a couple of bounds, staring at us in the characteristic stance of an alert kangaroo. She had an ethereal quality as the early morning sun caught her hide, turning her in the instant into burnished gold. Her beauty in that frozen moment was so complete that a sob of emotion forced the question into my mind: "Why? Why does man kill such beauty for so little gain?" The moment was magic. As I craned my neck to watch the kangaroo, she lost the shaft of sun, becoming mortal again. In that still frozen reality I heard a whisper of thought in the silence of my mind.

Our pain is the sickness of man. This will only end when man heals himself. He is sick, for he has no knowing of himself or the part he plays in life. Man stands alone — and very afraid.

The voices of Nature, which had slowly been entering my conscious awareness, deepened and strengthened, and with them grew the deep, subconscious, unreasonable fear. Nature began speaking from trees, from rocks, from the ocean, and from the river, particularly the river. The dream had triggered an upsurge of thought, far deeper and more profound than my own, which moved into my mind with immense power and clarity, yet — paradoxically — with silence and subtlety.

I both welcomed this movement and cringed from it in fear. My logic told me I was going insane, while my intuition suggested that, indeed, it was total sanity. I was caught in the powerful grasp of two opposing aspects of myself, with neither side relenting.

In 1982 I was a speaker at the One Earth Conference in Australia where Treenie and I met Linda Tellington-Jones, and, when she called to see us after the conference was over, she became an important catalyst in my life. During our conversation she talked of the most outrageous things – UFO's, space visitors, Nature, talking trees, inner guidance. You name it, and Linda could embrace it with her own brand of discretion.

Under her inspiration I found myself sharing dreams, experiences, and strange happenings that I had kept locked away inside myself for a long time. Just talking about the voices of Nature which persisted in calling for my attention, and finding myself totally accepted by a stranger, was an incredible release. Linda was an ideal catalyst. She precipitated a change which resulted in an incredible happening three days after her departure. It began following another special dream. I had dreamed this particular dream week after week for a long time. It was powerful in its symbolism, but each time I awoke, the dream was gone, erased from my memory without trace or recall. I was only left with a sense of despair.

The third night after Linda's departure, I once again dreamed my recurring dream, but on awakening I remembered it all in clear and exact detail. While I lay awake feeling disturbed, the dream strong upon my mind, I gradually became aware of a presence in our bedroom. Treenie was asleep, breathing softly and easily, while the room around me became increasingly vibrant with energy. Peering into the darkness I could see nothing, but the presence was electric with intensity and power. Calmness and trust flowed over me, quelling all fear. Stilling my probing mind, I framed a question in my thoughts: "Who, or what, are you?" Immediately these words flowed into my receptive mind.

If you need to identify me, know me as the Spirit of Change. You are aware now of having this dream many times, yet never have you retained or understood its meaning.

Relaxed, I lay quietly accepting the experience. An instant comprehension of the recurring dream was impressed in my mind. I understood with total clarity. The voice from the Silence continued.

A long time ago, six lifetimes to be exact, you were a botanist. While your talents for the physical aspects were only average, you were blessed with a unique rapport with the plant kingdom.

Time elapsed and your studies deepened until you reached a stage where you began to experience a spiritual bonding with your plant subjects. Into your mind would flow ideas and images, projecting you into realms of thought quite unexplored. Later, as you deepened in your love and trust of Nature, you began to hear a flow of words in your mind, and you realized that there was an Intelligence which could communicate through the kingdom of Nature. You took copious notes on this, and for the first time you began to tell your friends. At first you talked with discretion, but gradually, flushed with their admiration, you spoke to others, and word went around to all who would listen. This led to your downfall, for some who listened considered your words blasphemous. Soon you were exposed to ridicule, and, when opinion went against you, you were subject to more persecution, finally seized, and you died under torture.

Your name of that time is not important; it died with you, and your papers were destroyed. Before you died, however, the pain of suffering induced a change in you, and you died blaming a divine gift for your torment. Thus, a block was imposed in your unconscious mind, and through the following four incarnations it has remained, unrealized and unchallenged. In this life, you have chosen to remove that mental block and once again allow the spiritual union with Nature to reestablish and develop. You are now aware of why you could not remember a recurring dream which your Soul-Self projected forward, hoping to cause you to remember. The unconscious block was too strong, the fear too great. This fear has been the spur behind your doubts, causing you to question beyond reason, for fear of more torment and an ongoing agony.

You are now ready to know the truth. In your dream six

*years ago, the sound of a joyous universe echoed in your ears
and spun before your eyes. You experienced a divine truth.
Buried and hidden beyond the five senses of man, truth beckons
eternally to the human spirit. No longer need you fear persecution or torture. Humanity now enters a period of transition and
those who seek to "know" must have that chance. No matter
how humble the offering, it must be laid on the altar of truth.
All you need will be revealed as you move to deepen the bonding, and only by your efforts will it be so.*

The presence was gone, instantly departed, yet an energy
lingered in the room as I lay in awe of things unseen and of
unknown power. For the first time I understood my fear. The
death-threat feeling was based on reality. I had once died, not
because of communicating with Nature's inner reality, but
because I lived in a time when such an action was sorcery, for
which the penalty was death.

The Being had also referred to my earlier dream, and, as I
suspected, my dream was of reality. Lying awake, I was aware
that only by action could I resolve the fear and end the doubts.
As before, understanding a cause does not immediately change
the effect. I would face the fear by deepening my link with an
inner Nature.

For a time I had floundered, at a loss to find a way to present
the voices of Nature. But then, that day, I had followed Treenie's
suggestion and gone to the river flowing past our house and
asked for help, and help had been given.

The day after my visit to the river I took our rubbish to the
local dump, which was filled with tons of junk from our throw-
away world. Having disposed of the garbage, I strolled into the
surrounding bush—so different from the vegetation around our
home. Huge gum trees sucked all the moisture from the soil and
only sparse undergrowth scattered the deep, acid leaf litter. I
walked slowly on through the open bushland. It was a dull day,
and the small flock of birds passing noisily and swiftly overhead
made a brief splash of sound and color against the overcast sky.

My eyes followed them, while I called out in my thoughts: "Hello, you lucky birds. I rejoice in your freedom of flight."

They were gone in moments, but I remained powerfully aware of a sensation of many birds filling the air.

We greet you. We rejoice in your inner freedom. We rejoice in your new flight path. Remember, however, every freedom has its price to pay. Only the Swift can fly high and at immense speeds, united with the air. Yet the Swift cannot play with the Sparrow. The carefree, tumbling, bumbling play of the Sparrow is lost.

Thus also, for you, the challenge will be that as you soar with the Eagle on higher thermals, with wider vision, so will you lose the companionship of those who seek lower zones. This you must realize and with understanding allow to happen. Any pattern of thought which knows not the freedom of space will become a burden. There will be those who fly even higher. Be aware of your own flight path and let the winds of change be ever fresh on your face.

Despite the cloud-laden sky, the day became brighter as I stood listening to those subtle words. The bird energy slowly dissipated, while a breeze stirred the foliage of a wattle further along on my path.

The wattles were in full bloom. It was as though the sun itself had come to earth to dwell in the deep, golden blossoms smothering the small trees with light and beauty. Fragrance hung heavy in the softly stirring air, and, while inhaling the scent, thoughts of gratitude and love moved through my mind.

"How beautiful you are, my friend wattles, yet I could have walked past without noticing you had not those birds called my attention, so immersed was I in mundane thoughts. I feel as though I have known this land and you magnificent trees for a far greater span than just this lifetime."

We greet you, human friend. Long have we known your energy. Great is our rejoicing as we witness the fresh winds of change moving through your Being.

*Even your inner colors change as the patterns of your inner
Self dance to a new rhythm in life. This must now be part of
your daily movement: to recognize, greet, and listen to all forms
of Nature, from the lowly moss to the greatest tree. All share in
the one life, all dance to the same rhythm, all blend their notes
in the song of the universe. We rejoice, our brother, for soon that
song will blend into your pattern of color, and the doors of a
new and deeper sharing will be thrown wide open.*

As I walked on my way, I realized that it is not only the sun
which can make a day much brighter. How is it that we deny
ourselves an inner sun, shining through the silent words
of Nature?

O NCE TRIGGERED, my response to Nature became a daily
adventure, and I spent hours by the river writing the
events and words in my journal as each moment
unfolded. There was one section of the river with which I had an
amazing empathy. Just a hundred yards downriver the character
of the river changed, no longer offering the same deep connection. In the newness of my experience I needed all the help I
could get, and it was noon one day when my footsteps took me
again along the now-familiar track. Filtering through the leaves of
the trees, the sun danced in mottled patterns on my shoulders.

Scrambling down the steep bank to the river, I felt the
power—immense—waiting for me. For a moment I felt inadequate, a sense of the old, familiar fear, then it was gone, lost in
the surging consciousness filling all life around me. Even before
I reached my place on the rock, the words were moving clearly
and with undeniable force through my mind.

*As you sit on the rock by the river, be aware of the life
around you. The Kingfisher flashing color in the morning sun.
Fish jumping in the clean, washed river. The sun warm on your
shoulders. The Water Dragon watching from a rotting log, distrust in its eyes. Microbes teeming in the rotting log.*

Be aware of the life beyond that which you are. Each leaf bursts with the hidden energy of spring. The force of life makes its presence known in all the creatures around you. Life in life. Life upon life.

You listen to the silent song of my voice.

I have spoken to mankind from the beginning of your time.

In a cascade of sound I call to you from every waterfall. With loving embrace I hold your bodies in the waters of the earth and softly I whisper.

In endless ways I call you, but so seldom am I heard. Not with your ears may I be heard, but in your heart, your consciousness. So easily are you lost in the labyrinths of your dimension. Your minds seek always to compare. Light compares with dark, strong with weak. Always the polarity of opposites reveals the identity of your experience.

I have no opposite. You cannot listen to my inner voice and then compare. You may not gaze into my inner world and seek the comfort of opposites. Your reality must stretch. Your limits must be pushed back. The dimension of opposites is but one facet of the whole reality.

The five physical senses of humanity are both your freedom of expression and the walls of your prison. This need not be. Humanity has the ability to create. Creation is an expression of the power of visualization. Within this controlled, creative framework, you may open doors into the realms of Nature where I will meet you.

You need only open the door. I will be there. Alas, to open this door defies all but the few. There are those who step beyond the known boundaries, but you know them not. For the most part they have a wisdom which embraces silence. They sip from the nectar of more subtle kingdoms, yet they sip sadly. People such as these wish to share the nectar of their lives, but it has long been rejected. This time is coming to an end. Once again, humanity stands on the threshold of Nature's secret kingdom. The Kingdom of your own Being. A secret wide open to all mankind, yet hidden behind the veils of love, of wisdom, of integrity.

The flow of words ended, but the feeling of power was vast. I sat for a while just gazing into the rippling water. I had no words, nothing to say. I felt only a sense of awe for the unseen, the unknown, the immensity of life swirling and coiling around me.

The surge of life seemed heightened in my moments of sharing with an inner Nature, and the following morning I returned to the river, tentatively testing the water for the new season of swimming. It was cold, but pleasant. Climbing from the river, water streamed in fine rivulets from my body. I sat on the rock, aware it had been waiting for me. The sky was blue. It was a warm, breezy day. River and breeze seemed to merge at the water surface, and I felt a fine inner tension in myself, caught and shimmering with the play of light racing over the river.

For some reason I felt as though I had been summoned here, and I was tense with anticipation. To the river I said aloud, "Thank you for the joy of swimming in your waters. If I have a passion within Nature, it is cool, clear rivers."

It is good that you enjoy the water so much. We greet you, we—the River and the Breeze.

Is it not a Breeze which moves within the water's flow? Is it not moisture which rides the air as Breeze? Each has been given separation by the concept of being different movements. See the Oneness in life. The song of the birds which prey on insects and the night cry of those insects are One.

Life moves through form, changing in a vast continuum from physical to physical, on and on, yet never in isolation. Be with this movement.

Allow your inner Giant Being an ever-greater freedom. Mankind, with the greatest potential for the ultimate freedom, chooses instead to become isolated.

Move beyond your barriers, and by the intelligence and freedom of Self, perceive within Nature the inner nature of your own Being.

Several leaves fell from a tree overhanging the water. Round and round they spiraled in the breeze, finally alighting on the river caressingly; so gentle was the falling.

The energy was soft, swirling in distant undulation, yet the silent words were clear.

A leaf falls in the breeze onto the water's surface. Now begins the movement back to its original cellular form. Given a period of time, the base minerals of the vanished leaf will once again surge within new sap moving within another leaf on another tree. From leaf to leaf, yet does one know of the other? So it is with humanity. Does present Self know of previous Self? Thus it is with all life. The movement never ends. Mortality is but a single moment in infinity. Man is infinite, not on a physical scale, but in Spirit. Truth is infinite. Mankind has a mind which, once mastered, can span infinity to know its own truth. This is your challenge.

The words were too powerful, the challenge too great.

I stood up and, launching myself from the rock, dived into the river. It was too much. I could not handle what was offered. It was too big, I felt too small. A child with an imperial parent offering presents beyond reach. I swam in a fast overarm trying to relieve my tension. Maybe now was the time to quit. How could I keep writing this as it happened and expect acceptance? Yet somewhere within, I knew a greater challenge—could I accept my own experience? Standing alone was a scary thought, and, as I swam, the words of the birds filtered through my mind.

Be aware of your own flight path.

Suddenly all those words about the Swift and the Sparrow became clear and amplified. They spoke of here and now. This was the price which had to be paid.

I swam slowly, exhausted, back to the rock. I said nothing, but I could feel that all was known.

It felt as though a choir was singing, but the clear words were carried on the echoes of Silence.

Our relationship must change. No longer may you feel yourself as little brother or child. Nature/mankind is but one movement, each an echo of the other.

*For too long you have listened to our words fearfully, spas-
modically, with many blocks imposed. Always you have listened as a child to a parent. This has been a protection behind
which you've hidden. This is ended. You must claim your status
and willingly meet your destiny.*

*You must claim the voices of Nature as the nature of your
own Being. We are One. You/I are but one expression, even
though consciousness draws to its Self different realities. "WE"
speak in the Breeze. "WE" listen in the Breeze. From The
River—The Stone—The Tree, or a river, a stone, a tree, there is
no separation.*

*Intelligence uses all forms through which to express. This
is not mankind's privilege alone. You questioned in your mind
whether you should write these words, or share them. You were
concerned for your protection. If you need protecting, then
cease, as of this moment.*

*When you write, accepting your experience without fear,
you become a focus. This is not a focus of personality, or ego,
but a focus for the inner light, so that its beam may flicker into
the beyond, the unknown.*

*You cannot move beyond your subconscious barriers with-
out the aid of a powerful focus. Once focused, this beam of
inquiry shall illuminate new dimensions of Nature/Self.*

For a while I sat quietly trying to take it all in. I realized
that trying to remember everything, or even change anything,
was a useless exercise. I can only be who I am.

For an hour I was busy writing in my journal, the spring sun
mellow on my skin. My thoughts flickered and jumped. One
thing seemed certain: The Intelligence of Nature did not mince
words, but I felt rather unclear about the focus. Oh well, if a
focus is going to happen, it will happen. It appeared I was in very
capable hands.

Lost in thought, my attention was caught by a movement
in the river. Undulating like a shadow of thick smoke, a shoal of
several hundred tiny fish weaved in and out of a shallow depres-
sion in the rock close to where I was sitting. They rode the cur-

rents of water with the same natural grace as an eagle rides on the currents of air. Fascinated by them I asked, "Well, fish, do you have a voice? Do you have a source of wisdom which can speak with me?" In one united movement the fish vanished, lost in the shadow of rock. Well, I thought, that's clear enough. Like a magnet my awareness was drawn into the empty hollow. No fish were to be seen, but I became aware of energy which was of fish and much more. It was fish, river, stone . . . and endless sky.

I felt surprised. This was more than I expected.

Have I not just told you that Intelligence moves through all physical forms? Whereas form is separate in its physical identity, Intelligence is One.

"What do you call Intelligence?" I asked.

Intelligence "IS" . . . but you could call it God.

I understood. Words can only capture an essence of the experience. I understood. Like magic, the hollow in the rock was again filled with the shoal of tiny, striped fish.

2
October

A S A RESULT OF CONNECTIONS made at the One Earth Conference, Treenie and I were invited to give a number of workshops in various cities and locations. Most important of all, Andrea and Bernie Dunne invited us to give a one-day seminar at their beautiful home in the Blue Mountains of New South Wales.

Bernie and Andrea were caretakers of the Everglades, a garden owned by the National Trust. At the time, they were negotiating a lease, so they could have greater control and be more innovative.

Everglades is one of the best-known gardens open to the public in New South Wales. The development of these outstanding gardens began in 1932 when Henri Van de Velde acquired the former ten-acre fruit orchard for a weekend retreat. By the time of his death in 1947, the gardens had been hailed as "an epic on the scale of a Wagner Opera." With the assistance of landscape designer Paul Sorensen and a small work force, Van de Velde carved wide terraces with superb dryrock stone walls. The visitor can see some of the world's outstanding trees and shrubs growing, in a quite breathtaking manner, alongside native Australian bush.

IT WAS IN THIS OUTSTANDING SETTING we were to hold our workshop, among the "vibes" of loved and cared-for plants. During the evening prior to our workshop, Andrea and Bernie took us for a walk around the gardens and into the immediately surrounding bush. The energies of the gardens and the bush mixed and merged with one another. The essential quality of the gardens was one of exaltation. It may sound strange, but it felt as though something was knocking on a closed door, and, although I did not know what the something was, I knew I was the closed door. But . . . I was keen to open myself.

When we walked down into the Grotto, the heightened feeling surged powerfully, and I knew I must return soon alone. As I followed in Andrea's footsteps, two other areas also heightened this feeling to dizzying proportions. I determined that the next morning I would make a dawn rendezvous with the mysterious "something."

THE GROTTO WAS A DEEP, natural amphitheater, gouged from the earth in an ancient past. It was a place of stillness, invoking a sense of awe for the surrounding beauty of Nature. A trickle of water seeping from the deep pool at my feet fell with a persistent melody into the unwinding waterway, vanishing in the scrub downhill. Early-morning birds, including the laughing Kookaburra, sang their ritual greetings to the rising sun. I watched the wavering sky and rippling trees reflected in the dark water, as a breeze played over the surface. Allowing time for my mind to quiet, I felt a powerful inverted energy around me, as though it had been coiled and waiting for millennia. The contorted lava walls of the Grotto bulged protectively around the pool, while mosses, ferns, and creeping violets clambered in profusion over every crack and convoluted crevice. It was a scene of tranquility and beauty. For a while I listened to the trickling waterfall below me, allowing myself time to identify with the mysterious energy of the Grotto. Quietly, not wishing to disturb the fragile silence, I spoke to the reflective water.

"I feel privileged to be here. Just to sit within your Silence is a nourishment. I have no questions. It is enough to be here and to be open to life."

Strange as it may seem, each time I connect with the Intelligence of Nature on this level I am aware of a difference in feeling when words flow into my mind. Just as we have our different character, so the energies of Nature differ in subtle ways. Thus, in this grotto the energy had its own character: In our way of thinking, it was alone, yet it knew nothing of isolation.

Be welcome. By no accident are you here. People from many aspects of life find their way to this pool. It is a place where barriers are laid aside and defenses dropped. It is here that many people are able to "feel" the essence of Nature for the first time.

The feeling beyond form.

For these people allow the first chink of light to penetrate their ironclad belief systems. I am a focus of energy, a container which will shatter with perfect timing, and my energy will be realized.

I feel your bewilderment at my suggestion.

Understand that we are entering a time of change. Each one of your kind is a container of spiritual energy, but unfortunately you have no knowing of the energy you contain. "You are" the contained. We, the expressing energies of Nature, know our place in the grand design of life.

You are aware that you listen and talk, not with the stone and water forming the physical foundation of the Grotto, but with the collective intelligent energy residing here.

Again you are aware I am not physical. Only the container is physical, as your appreciative eyes can see. Thus it is with your kind. Your bodies are merely physical containers of Spirit.

You are rediscovering your latent ability to unite with the energies of earth. There is no limit to the range of this power. It is universal, all-encompassing. This, my friend, is the journey you are undertaking. Eventually you will be more clear about the purpose.

Gaze into the depths of this water and you will see reflected what is all around you. Equally, when you view all life around you directly, you see but a reflection of the real world. Life for humanity is living within this hazy and distorted reflection. Yet each of you has the ability to perceive life as it is and take loving dominion. This requires an energy humanity lacks — humility. Humility is the creative power of the universe, contained, knowing its place in the design of life. With or without the help of mankind, this design unfolds, but that which could have been fulfillment becomes a senseless pain. My friend, just as I have blended energies with you, so I blend with all who visit here. Each is aware according to his or her own level of perception. The love I feel and share with you, I feel in all your kind. It is the expression of this love which must be guided along a path of wisdom. We are united in Spirit.

Go in peace.

I lingered for a while, but knowing my schedule I could not delay overlong. The peacefulness was pervading and mysterious.

Following the normal footpath to a large, smooth boulder, I left the track, pushing my way through the undergrowth to a small cavern, or, to be more precise, a rocky overhang.

When we visited here the previous evening a small Boobook Owl watched us from a branch only a few yards from where we stood; its large, unblinking eyes regarded us without fear, reflecting our admiration with mystic gaze. Now, in my early morning visit, the owl had returned from its night hunting, and, as I sat in this serendipitous cavern, it carefully went through a routine of meticulously cleaning feathers and claws. Crouching close to the rock face at the rear of the cavern, I regarded my surroundings as only a plant lover could, torn between a desire to own it all and an even stronger appreciation for its perfect natural artistry. Clambering up the back of the cavern was a green fitted carpet of moss, covered with small creeping ferns extending furry, orange squirrel's feet into ready nourishment among the damp and tangled vegetation. Allowing an inner perception to flood beyond my physical experience, I became vaguely disoriented. I extended an unvoiced inquiry. From within the rock walls and myself came the words:

Long have you shared this land with our kind, and long have you forgotten your own ancient past. You have been drawn to this particular place, which you shall remember.

You shall remember the time, so long ago measured by the span of lives, when you walked this land. Let your dreams remember, and in your dreaming know the symbols not in your head, but in your heart. This is where the Dreaming lies.

Heart connects with heart, for it is here the spirit of mankind resides. In dreaming shall you awaken. Allow your ancient lineage to reappear, for your past and future are with this moment, entwined.

Time is the weaver of the illusion mankind believes is life.

I crouched against the rocks, painfully aware of my physical discomfort. The little owl watched with unconcerned interest as I stretched my limbs. Timelessness pervaded the cavern, wrapping me in a shroud of clouded mystery. I could feel an aboriginal man standing near me, but also a vastly older man who was neither black nor white. My sense of perception peered foggily into scenes from bygone ages. In a manner which was neither visual nor physical, I was aware of tracing myself back and back into time. It was as though the cavern contained an inner, subtle history of mankind—a natural book waiting to be opened and experienced according to the inner dictates of the searcher. I asked the question bubbling in my mind.

"How can history be stored here? How can I be shown my own past in a place I am not aware of ever having visited?"

The atmosphere became imbued with a sense of unlimited, endless space.

Relax. You are linking with your own past, trekking through the illusion of time into other phases of your own Self. You are being led to locations which you have frequented in another time. Physically much has changed, yet despite this you cannot go anywhere or be anywhere without leaving the imprint of Being.

My head reeled. The concept which was forming in my mind was surely preposterous.

"Do you mean to suggest that in the way a fingerprint on a hard surface leaves an impression, we leave an impression by just having occupied a space in the atmosphere?"

Clearly and powerfully came the reply.

That is exactly what I mean. You cannot perform a physical act, or think a thought that is not recorded.

The inner journey you have taken in this cavern will continue and extend, in times of stillness, in your Dreaming. I will guide you. Our consciousness is linked. You shall know me as the Keeper of the Cavern, and in time you will know the true meaning of "The Cavern."

The slumbering Giant within the Dwarf awakes.

You may leave. Whether you return to this place physically or not is unimportant, for as I contain you, so also do you contain me.

This is known and recognized.

I had been through too many strange inner experiences to be more than momentarily disturbed. I was aware that I was on this journey only because, after years of resistance, I was finally allowing a powerful inner reality to emerge.

As I crawled from the cavern into bright sunlight, the owl's head swiveled smoothly around to follow my progress.

"Well," I said, "do you have some wise thoughts to offer?"

The owl merely stared at me, unblinking.

Forcing my way through the tangled undergrowth, I glanced at my watch. I felt a sense of shock. My experience in the cavern had seemed no more than ten minutes, yet well over an hour had passed. I had one more destination before I left this enchanted garden, and, after finding the winding track, I clambered over an outcrop of smooth yet convoluted granite overlooking the gully. Scattered trees grew from precarious rootholds around me, while far below in the gully the fresh foliage of the treetops swayed and danced in the eddying breeze.

An energy, wide open, expansive, and of light-filled proportion, swept around and through me, while an inner voice boomed, hale and jovial.

Greetings. Do you not feel the urge to jump from these rocks and fly?

The distant sound of water trickling in a thin cascade from the nearby grotto seemed to be amplified, filling the air with liquid notes, bright and inviting. I admitted flying free was exactly what I felt like doing, but I knew it could not be. A vast chuckle filled all space around me.

But you are jumping, my friend. You are testing the strength of your newfound wings. You are learning to soar on inner thermals, for this is the gift of mankind. A neglected gift. Neither airplane nor rocket will ever cover the space that your kind can reach on inner levels. All that lies before you and beyond is but a reflection of inner space in the "real" world.

Cast not your physical body from these rocks, but let your mind soar, carried on the safe wings of wisdom onto the higher, rarer thermals. Fly, my friend, fly.

All mankind will benefit as each individual finds the doorway to their inner freedom. We are linked not only cell for cell, body for body, but in the inner reaches of space we fly as One. Reach in, my friend, reach out, and fly. There is nothing else you can do. To resist will be pain, to delay will abort. To fly the inner space and expand is all that is left.

A sense of elation filled me, of vastness and expansion. Leaping to my feet on a surge of energy, I shouted aloud, "THANK YOU—OH THANK YOU," hurling my voice over and beyond the gully, hearing the sound echo and bounce from the rocks before being smothered and swallowed by the surrounding trees. Then I noticed the early-morning tourists who, having heard my outcry, were regarding me on the distant rock as though I were some rare species. I felt no embarrassment—caught as I was in such unseemly behavior.

The day was just too much . . . too much!

I found it rather difficult to bring myself down to earth for the morning workshop, for while my spirit soared, my mind was required in a discussion on the implications and applications of organic farming. After lunch, in a change of mood, we used Nature as the pivot for a discussion on self-awareness, which brought forth greater attention and concentration among the participants.

The seminar over, we continued our tour into Sydney and then on to Canberra where we stayed a few days with Bridget Hodgkin, a very dear friend. Elderly, active, and intelligent, Bridget, with her keen humor and wonderful hospitality, was a highlight in our travels. On our way home Treenie and I discussed the various aspects of our tour, easily reaching the conclusion that my presentation at the Everglades was not a true reflection of my inner feelings. It seemed that although I spoke of organic concepts with conviction and feeling, my heart, my drive, my inspiration lay with a deeper movement, a movement into the heart of Nature. We decided that I would speak only where and when I could share this inner reality: that each movement has its own moment, but only with perfect timing. Now was the time of my inner journeying, of gaining greater insight and clarity, rather than speaking from vague and unfamiliar concepts.

The warmth and friendliness of home was most welcome; even the trees reached out and extended themselves to us, especially the Morton Bay Fig. Each time we open the back door of our house, we are greeted by the outspread branches of this enormous tree. This is no ordinary tree. It is a giant whose massive limbs stretch out to embrace the surrounding countryside. Here, amid the large dark-green leaves, hang the bunches of small tart-flavored fruit which attracts Yellow Fig birds, Catbirds, Bowerbirds, and many other varieties by day, while the constantly swearing Flying Foxes are lured in great numbers on summer nights. Only when the fruit is no longer in season is the tree quiet, silently contemplating its surroundings. Standing beneath the wide spread of this mammoth tree invokes a feeling of humility; the ego is dwarfed to insignificance. The personality of this tree reaches into all who gaze upon it, and few can pass by unmoved.

Talking to such a tree is easy. The very grandeur invites conversation. I would no more walk beneath the branches on my way to the river without a word of greeting than you would pass your family pet without a word of recognition. I find it strange that whereas conversation with the family pets is considered normal and taken for granted, the resonance and joy of our trees and plants are unrecognized. One morning, on my way to the river, I mentioned this to the tree. Its massive buttress root system spread almost as far as its branches. I placed my towel on a convenient, comfortable root and sat down for a chat.

"Mr. Morton Bay Fig—Sir or Madam, as the case may be—can you tell me, from your infinite source of wisdom, why it is that we humans talk to cats and dogs, even horses, goats, pigs, and any number of animal pets, never receiving a verbal reply or even expecting one, yet we seldom talk to trees or other plants or rocks or rivers?"

The voice of my friend the Tree was clear, ringing like a gigantic bell in my receptive mind.

I feel your humor and your sense of joy. I nderstand the source. During your recent journey you released more attachments to mental burdens, expanding your awareness of the inner realms of Nature. I will give your flippant question serious consideration, for it indicates a point of change in human consciousness. There is now a rapidly increasing number of people who do indeed talk to trees and other plants.

This has been difficult for the present race of man to embrace. You talk to your animals with ease, feeling an empathy within the animal kingdom, for this is the kingdom in which mankind identifies himself.

From a human viewpoint, the plant kingdom is beneath you; thus, you fail to realize that mankind is a synthesis of the mineral, vegetable, and animal kingdoms. Your reasoning minds experience the plant kingdom as having no emotion or conscious intelligence. This failing to experience and under-stand a truth does not change truth; it merely limits your abil-ity to relate to life as it "IS" rather than as you see it.

As a new era dawns, your race, in order to survive, will dis-cover that the Nature perceived outside of your Selves is but a reflection of your own inner nature. This connection with a greater realization is being felt by many people, even as you now experience it.

My flippancy had faded, but the feeling of joy and fun was even stronger. "Thank you, Tree, Sir or Madam. I have no argu-ment with what you share; I only wish more people could experience such a conversation as this. It is obvious to me that we should all branch out into having tree friends, or potted-plant pals."

Laughing aloud I bounded to my feet, heading for the river. I was well clear of the tree when the thinnest of far-flung roots caught my toe and sent me sprawling. The tree had the last laugh . . . Sir or Madam, as the case may be!

A T AN EARLY AGE I had turned to the solitude and Silence of Nature. In the quietness of field, hedgerow, and the banks of many streams, I had studied the movements of Nature, relaxed, trusting my environment.

In those quiet moments, precious as living jewels, I would daydream of the way life could be, of inner strengths I would love to have.

Early in life I had developed a rage against being born. Birth had been an extremely painful imposition. No easy entry for me. By the time I had started school, from seven to fourteen years of age, I had been a chronic rebel. Any imposition or discipline was a target for my inner rage, and the private school which I attended, where the cane and thrashing were accepted punish-ments, was a very unfortunate affair.

Discipline was strictly imposed, and the harsh, eccentric head teacher was a person to be feared. My inner rage flared into perpetual rebellion at the violence and condescending attitude of those teachers and their system of teaching. The years of battle, of matching wits with my teachers, profoundly altered my life. Those teachers, unwittingly or not, insulted and outraged my intelligence and sense of fair play. They ignited in me a distrust of authority, discipline, and regimentation, but I found I could trust Nature, that here I was always welcome, that some inner chamber of my heart seemed to open, and in the opening I was enriched. This never seemed to happen in my contact with people, only with Nature.

My mind was disinterested in proven avenues of thought. Instead, like a renegade, it burrowed deep into the folds of imagination, undisciplined and untrained. The eight years of my school life were a bore, a burden; while in the silence and solitude of Nature, a totally different experience stirred both my interest and my imagination.

A single compensation during my school life was the nearby Botanical Gardens. After school I would leap onto my bicycle and tear around to this wonderful diversion. Like a bee to nectar, I would be drawn to the hothouses. The gardens were owned by Cambridge University. Magnificent glasshouses covered quite a large area, and their hot, steamy air welcomed me time and time again. Strange, contorted flowers from weirdly shaped plants clambered and crept in an ordered profusion from benches and beds. My eyes, round and staring in my efforts to absorb everything, grew familiar with every plant growing there. From the very first visit, it was a love affair with an exotic Nature.

It had been preordained that, as a scholastic incompetent, I would work for my father on the land, while my older brother, a scholastic genius, would go on to the university at Cambridge. At fifteen I left school, and my love affair with Nature ended. Gone were the lonely, unstructured wanderings of my youth. In their place emerged the rigid doctrine of agriculture. Gone was the wonder, the awe, the tinge of reverence. Instead, a pre-ordered cycle of sow and reap was imposed upon me. The spontaneity I had known was crushed beneath growing responsibility. The wildness of daisy-filled meadows and sweet-flowing streams, of majestic woods and cold, silent waters gave way to the harsh reality of plowing and sowing, crop spraying and harvesting. Over and over, year in, year out. It was a ritual which I both loved and hated.

Although I loved the connection with Nature, I instinctively hated the arrogant approach of dominance. Intuitively I recoiled from the alienation between Nature and agriculture. Such was the routine, the work load, the endless seasons of repetition that the inner flame of my early connection with Nature gradually diminished to a faint glimmer. It was a subtle imposition. I labeled the chains of bondage as freedom, that I might survive. Fooling myself with this grand illusion, I forged my way through life for the next thirty years, believing myself to be free; yet, even though I hugged this cloak of deceit around me in hidden, subconscious despair, light and true freedom burned brightly within, ensuring that, with the years, my ordered life would collapse, revealing another way, another path that I might walk.

Leaving school had robbed me of the innocence of my earlier experience with Nature, an innocence which could never be recaptured. However, there was always one favorite refuge — that of Byron's Pool Woods. They were near Granchester, ancestral home of the famous poet Lord Byron, and were only a few minutes' cycle ride from where I lived. Byron's Pool Woods — the words still echo in my heart as a thrill, a lingering memory, rich in detail. Byron's Pool Woods were a mecca for Nature lovers, abounding in history and mystery. On the fringe of the woods lay a large, river-fed pool. Under about four to five feet of water, the foundations of the old Mill House could be dimly seen. We kids could wade to this foundation on one side, but the other side dropped away into deep water. I learned to swim from these old foundations, submerged in the cold, dark waters of Byron's Pool.

A weir close by, green with algae, regulated the water in times of winter flood, but in summer, in our swimming weather, only a trickle of water flowed over the wide platform behind the old, hand-cranked watergates. Hour upon hour I sat there alone, staring into the water. Rivers, streams, creeks—they have always held a fascination, a bond I cannot easily explain. Whenever I was in the lonely company of a river I would feel the pull of a great longing—a longing I neither understood nor even fully realized.

Somehow, in the heart of a youth a connection developed, a spontaneous linking with Nature. Whatever that connection was, it transcended physical barriers. That which was born in me as a boy had now reemerged, sparkling, fresh with invitation. I was encouraged to pursue an inner truth, a dream where my connection with Nature became alive, activated, where I was no longer alone, but consciously connected with all life.

I WAS EIGHTEEN when I was inveigled by a friend into going on a Church Youth Camp holiday with him. It was there I met Treenie—she stood out from the rest of the giggling girls, and I was instantly attracted to her. I deviously changed the duty roster, and we eventually met over the breakfast dishes, our hands touching in the frothy soap suds. I say in all modesty, Treenie was swept off her feet!

The sun shone every day, inside and out. Britain had the hottest summer in several years, and Treenie and I wandered the countryside and walked the beaches of Robin Hood Bay. We fell in love—a love which over the years has endured, grown, expanded, and blossomed.

3
November

A T FAIRLY REGULAR INTERVALS I have enjoyed walking into our nearby semitropical rain forest. Usually this is a very physical affair, where I can admire Nature's amazing creations for their physical value and intrigue. I was feeling now that I would like to take a walk in the forest, relating in a different way to my environment. Nature was indicating that there are many levels of expression beyond the physical – the formless beyond the form – and I wanted to find out if I could push back the barriers in my own way. I had a sneaky feeling that I could only go so far or fast, rather like a car responding to fuel and throttle, with a driver in charge. I needed to find out if I was car – driver – or both!

I have a theory that when I was born, hauled forth with clamps on my head, that the pressure (which I have learned is considerable) caused an abnormality to my brain. Don't laugh! I am quite serious about this. I have yet to meet anyone with a worse sense of direction than me. I get lost in department stores. Supermarkets are an unbelievable hazard. I must be the only adult who gets handed in to the lost children's center! By now you can see the picture I am trying to present. I could get lost among a dozen trees. Can you imagine me in a forest? So, rather than create a situation where Treenie is required to keep a

Bloodhound or Retriever, I generally go with one or another of my close friends — someone who can listen to me talking to trees or rocks, without thinking I have them in my head. One fine, sunny day my good friend Gerhard and I set out on an exploratory, tree-talking trip into the forest. As would be expected, Gerhard is a born Nature lover. He is slight of build, medium height, and his sensitive green eyes which gaze from a bearded face are forever roaming over the trees and the ground, absorbing the finer aspects of Nature. For him, bush walking is a love affair, an extension of his love for all things wild. His companionship on such walks is perfect. He knows intuitively when I need to be alone, fading away quietly to concentrate on his own areas of interest.

The rocky gorge was just one of many on the forest-covered foothills plunging from the New England Plateau. Large boulders torn from the towering escarpment littered the gorge, while a clear, cold stream plunged heedlessly through the semitropical profusion of trees smothering its course. I sat on a small, comfortable rock facing a huge boulder which loomed above and beyond the other. A thick mat of moss covered much of the surface, creating perfect conditions for the magnificent Bird's Nest Ferns dotted upon it. Life on the boulder was lived in almost perpetual shade and moisture, a perfect microclimate. On inner levels I felt the boulder growing to immense proportions, the ferns rearing like trees in my consciousness. I sent a thought of invitation, of recognition, to this huge boulder and the residual energy it encompassed. Water gushing around and over the rocks filled the air with sound, while the nearby Cicadas picked it up, amplifying it with enthusiasm. Through all the noise of a living, vibrant gorge, the voice of rock consciousness spoke clearly.

You are welcome. We welcome an attitude of respect and admiration. For too long the forests have been exploited to meet your needs on a physical level. It is time now to merge our energy with mankind on higher, finer levels.

With noise from water and Cicadas competing for my attention, I was having trouble concentrating. The words flowed into my mind and all sound was outside the experience, but I was being distracted.

Do not resist the sound of water, the sounds of life. As a breeze moves through the unresisting leaves of a tree, thus should you drop your resistance.

Allow the inner energy of this stream to pour through your inner Being as a purification. There is a uniqueness expressing itself here. Each area of the gorge has its own different essence. Each area has its own uniqueness to offer mankind.

I was puzzled by this. After all, a stream is a stream and a gorge is a gorge. How could it be one and different at the same time?

"Are you suggesting that water energy from the river here is different when it reaches the valley? How can this be so when logically it is the same water?"

My friend. In Nature, only the physical reflection you see as your world will stand up to the scrutiny of logic. You are learning to perceive, and integrate with, a finer world, a higher truth. I would ask you in reply: If mankind formed a line several miles long, would the character of the mile remain unchanged?

The concept was a new one, yet I got the point. A human line, while being all human, would be composed of as many identities as it took to make up the line. That such a concept would be applied to a gorge or river had never occurred to me. But why not? The river flowing past our home came into my mind. Of course! I was aware of how I felt a change in energy from my favorite place to other sections of the river. Certainly "my" area of river is unique. Why should this not apply to rivers, creeks, and water courses generally? The thought was an odd one. Many questions surfaced in my mind, becoming more and more confused with logic and reason. I struggled to balance the physical and metaphysical realities.

I felt a ripple shudder through the boulder's consciousness ... a very faint mockery.

So much you ask, so much you need to encompass. Forget

*your questions based on logic and knowledge. Soak instead in
the stream of higher energies. See, feel, inquire beyond physical
form, and your knowing, like a waterfall, will fill you with the
cascade of truth with perfect timing.*

Leaving the boulder in the gorge, we journeyed on to eventually emerge from the dense, tropical undergrowth onto a high
ridge overlooking our destination: the waterfall.

Standing on the ridge, we were dwarfed by huge trees forming a natural corridor a hundred yards in length. Hoop Pines,
Stringy Bark, Brush Box, and other giants formed the pillars of
Nature's forest cathedral, while the waving foliage, high above
our heads, formed the ceiling. A hush holding the place in its
grip invoked a feeling of reverence, a knowing that one careless
shout could shatter the magic. On inner levels I could feel energies surging, intangible, but clearly active. Moving from this
collective power, the words entered my mind.

*It is good that you visit these places. Always we welcome
those who walk among us with love in their hearts.*

*It is wise that you come to attune, to respect, and admire.
Respect and reverence may become the doorways to higher
realities of Nature.*

*It is only by softly knocking on the doors with humility
that attunement may be slowly achieved.*

*Learn to know your Self and to understand what it implies
to be human, for there is much to realize. Just as each tree has
roots which are forerunners, so each age of this planet has its
sentient race.*

Can you, for just one moment, realize that today's humanity is but the forerunner of another race of man?

*Yet this shall come to pass when from the ruins of each
civilization mankind again emerges. Many times this has happened, and many times will it be repeated. In each age, mankind reaches a peak of power. Always, man has chosen the
power of destruction. Thus, as a tree grows true to seed, man
reaps the seed he has sown. Only when mankind reaches a high*

peak of wisdom will this cycle end. At this point a new emphasis shall emerge.

In our present cycle man has once again reached a time where he holds in his grasp the seed of his destruction. This shall cause both the beginning and the end.

The words left me feeling rather troubled and silent. I did not like the ominous overtones, and I was too close to the experience to be objective. Getting to my feet from the log on which I had been sitting, I walked over to a nearby Hoop Pine and hugged it.

"Is it as bad as it sounds?" I asked.

I heard nothing, but a clarity swept through me. It was as though a negative focus had suddenly switched off to be flooded with the illumination of a positive force. I had listened to words of hope, of life, of continuity. The end "is" the beginning, the beginning "is" the end; for on a spiral, life is cycles in an infinite continuum. We cannot take a finite view of infinity and make it fit; thus, our thinking must spiral out and expand. "Thank you," I whispered to the pine.

As we walked down toward the waterfall, I felt the energy on the ridge form into a vast phoenix, rising high above the trees, triumphant and free. From hundreds of yards above my head, water plummeted down the rock face, pouring into the deep, cold pool at my feet. We were fringed by trees. Hoop Pines clustered along the perimeter of the rock face. Liana clambered carelessly over the various trees, their huge looping vines resembling coiled serpents from a legendary past. Within this sheltered, secluded place, hidden in the surrounding forest, the summer sun shone warm upon the water, highlighting a misty halo of beauty from the cascading falls. Blood seeped steadily from my several leech bites into the pool, but there was humor in the situation. The leeches had been at "one" with my body. I had little compassion for their welfare as I pulled them—gorged and bloated on my blood—from my ankles. I accepted, however, that they were doing their thing—very effectively. I was not victimized. I was merely a walking blood bank.

A cool wind, created by the downpouring water, cooled the sweat on my brow. I gazed longingly at the cold water in which I intended to numb my hundreds of mosquito bites. Despite cord trousers and shirt I had been bitten on legs, shoulders, arms, and neck each time I stopped to write in my journal. It is ironic, for my attunement is not with the separate physical form, but only with the intelligent energy expressing through that particular form as a species. Unfortunately, I am as yet offered no protection from the physical, even while conversing with the psychical.

Once, about a year ago, when sun bathing on a river beach in late summer, I asked a large, interested, uninvited March Fly not to bite. Immediately I felt an upsurge of March Fly energy and, despite an equal surge of doubt, I heard the words formed in my then-skeptical mind.

The fly cannot do as you ask. Such a creature knows nothing of free will. The fly is a life-form following a strictly imprinted code of behavior, and this only may it do. Part of this code is to draw blood from warm-blooded mammals for nourishment.

I ask you, is it possible to view such as this fly with tolerance, understanding, and even love? Such an attitude would have two effects. One, it reduces drastically the chance of being the fly's victim; two, it cancels completely the chance of being a victim of your own separation and resulting lack of understanding.

Some fly!

By the pool, with blood seeping copiously from my leech bites, I assumed the same principle applied. My attention was drawn to the cascading falls. To attempt a description would deny the waterfall its true beauty. I can write only of its magnificence, yet it is more, for it has another quality. The fall invokes a magnetic attraction, not in the physical sense, but in ways which draw my thoughts and feelings at odd moments of the day. Aloud, and within the thunder of cascading turbulent water, I spoke to the waterfall.

"Thank you, waterfall. Thank you for inviting me here again. Thank you for making me feel I am a part of Nature, rather than apart from Nature. What is different about this waterfall? What attracts me and others beyond the physical beauty?"

The inner energy of waterfall became vast. All physical limits were suddenly abandoned, as in an inner world this waterfall became all that "IS." It contained me, and it was I who poured down the rock face, yet I contained it, watching with loving interest.

I welcome you both. Be aware; remember I am not the waterfall, you are not the hand which writes. Observe the difference, and the similarity. You are Intelligence which seeks expansion, which seeks its own destiny — to know its Self.

That I am also.

It is in this sense of Wholeness that we leave behind our attachment and identity with physical form, to merge as "One" consciousness. For my energy this is the reality of life; for you, the physical identity is that which you believe to be you, an attachment created over millenia. It is a powerful thought-form and belief from which to break away, yet this must be your challenge.

This waterfall is a focus of energy. Many other waterfalls focus power to a lesser or greater degree, but it is always subtle, normally beyond the perception of mankind.

For a while I dived and swam in the clear, cold pool. The words and the experience had faded, but not the subtle beauty of the wilderness surrounding me. Like a doll on the cliff top, Gerhard yodeled from far above, his voice faint in the thunder of water.

Some time later, when he had joined me, I shared my experience with him. He was quiet for a while, his eyes holding a faraway look.

"I feel what you are saying. I am not good with words, but when I stand at the waterfall I just feel this is all the Song of our Creator. It brings me to such a feeling of happiness. I become balanced. I am content. I feel that everything which 'IS,' I am. I belong to the rocks and the water. Such a feeling—exultation. Even God couldn't feel better."

Not good with words, he said!

E ARLY ONE MORNING, while the first rays of sunshine were probing the mists, banishing the delicate moisture to the higher atmosphere, I walked down toward the river. For no particular reason, except maybe the cloud of flies which accompanied me, I made for a different location and sat at the river's edge on a fallen log in deep shade. It was a smart move, for the flies were still seeking warmth from the early sun, and they quickly deserted me. My thoughts turned to my mother living on the other side of the world. It saddened me that with age she was becoming increasingly burdened with arthritis and was unlikely to gaze on such a scene as lay before me. A family of Plovers flew past, chattering with harsh cries as they followed the river. I detected no alarm from them as their cries greeted the new day. Mullet were leaping from the river, while freshwater Herring tried hard to excel their larger rivals, flashing quicksilver in the early sun. A Fantail flew from across the river, alighting on the log within a hand's reach. She regarded me for moments with beady eye and waving tail, undecided whether I posed a threat. With a final flick of tail feathers the bird departed, silent, yet noisy in presence.

The morning had opened gloriously. I was filled with a desire to roll up this wonderful natural scene, contain this magic moment, place it in a small, neat package, and send it to my mother in England, that she might share this privileged joy. Just imagine! On opening the parcel she unrolls it to find a slice of Australia's finest scenery before her eyes. She would see a clear, sparkling river, fresh from the recent rains, complete with leaping, gleaming fish, with Plovers and Fantails enriching this magic scene. River Oak and Weeping Willows would jostle for position along one bank, while smooth river stones formed a friendly beach on the other side. My mother would hear the gurgling chuckle of the water as it left the slow, silent river depths and raced splashing and noisy over the shallow, stony bed, while the whispered sound of a Kingfisher flashed electric blue as it hit the water, adding richness and quality to Nature's gift.

Dew, hanging in glistening beads from countless blades of grass, reflected in each drop a tiny rainbow, richer by far in its newness than any coveted jewel, symbolic of crystallized age – all this my mother would see. Somehow I know that while I gaze upon this beauty, holding fond memories of Mother in my heart, then in the secret recess of her soul this gift is known, this moment shared.

For a while I sat in the shade, memories of my mother and father moving through my mind. Certain episodes were of joy and happiness, while others filled me with regret, yet always the stamp of inevitability lay over everything, as though destiny will have its way no matter what. Are we free to choose? Or are we free to choose within no choice at all?

If we live in a framework of cause and effect, then must we reap effect before we can change cause to change effect? In other words, is choice predetermined by cause of the past, and thus preordained to no choice at all? The shade was moving soundlessly away when I left the log to walk back to the house for breakfast. After closing the paddock gate, I paused at our shadehouse where row upon row of Cycad palms completely dominated one bench. As I walked into the shadehouse looking at the young palms, my reflective mood carried me back again, this time into the forest where I came across the parent Cycad Palm or, as it is locally known, Burrawong Palm. These are not at all uncommon, yet this particular palm had a large, cone-shaped pod growing from its center. A tentative pull and the seed pod was in my hands, all fifty pounds of it.

Each seed was the size of a large chestnut, and all 150 seeds were bulky and heavy on the strong, thick stem. Accepting the help of my accompanying friends, we wrapped the spiky pod in my shirt, taking turns to carry it home. Within weeks the seed fell away from the pod, revealing each to be a vivid and unexpected orange color. The seed were then placed in close-packed rows on several shallow trays of forest soil. Their bright color quickly faded to a dull brown, and they lay apparently lifeless for the next eighteen months. The pod was collected on Easter Sunday in April, and it was November the following year when long tap roots burst from the dormant seed. For Treenie and me it heralded activity as we began the task of potting them in large, plastic plant bags. While working we were both aware of a subtle energy emanating from the plants, indicating their vigor and abundant vitality. Despite having no more than a single root when we potted them, in a few weeks the first palm fronds were reaching toward the light as the nutlike seed sent forth their stored energy. Under normal circumstances most seed on the forest floor would be chewed and eaten by animals, or in later stages riddled and bored by insects. Indeed, few of the hundreds would grow to mature palms. Under our conditions most of the seed were now sprouting, beginning their very slow growth toward large and handsome palms. Speculating on the energy of the plants I sent my first thought of inquiry toward their intelli gent consciousness.

"What is your place in the scheme of things?" I asked.

Come over here.

It was unmistakably a command and I felt a keen sense of surprise. I had expected the focus of Cycad energy to be with the plants laid out before me. Instead, the command, although within my consciousness and therefore unrelated to physical space, was directly behind me, coming from a couple of large Cycads growing in the shade of a Rubber tree in our garden.

I walked over to the palms and sat down before them.

"Okay," I responded, "here I am."

There was a feeling of outpouring energy, rather as though the presence of Cycad had heightened and intensified.

Your question has no real meaning. Our energy on physical levels is not as important in this age as it once was. We are of an ancient order and our lineage as a palm dates back a long way in objective time.

Once, in a bygone past, our energy played a vital role in the transition of form for many species of plants.

I digested this in silence.

"It has felt very important for us to grow these Cycads. I am not sure why we feel so strongly about it. Suddenly it occurs to me: Did you have anything to do with this whole episode?"

It is not by accident you grow our species and foster our energy. We represent a great age of plants and infinite change. Our species has seen animals and birds evolve and disappear. We are linked to this ancient consciousness, for although it no longer manifests in a physical sense, consciousness cannot cease to be. Understand this. We link with the energy of extinct forms. Through us you also may link with the consciousness of discarnate Nature.

This linking will be subtle, very subtle, yet there will be a stirring of unconscious memories. To the surface of the mind, long-forgotten connections with your ancient past will reemerge.

This linking is of great importance. Although the repercussions of your act will not be known to you, allow your mind to dwell on the concept of linkage, the past with the present, the present with the future. Imagine this all rolled into one sphere, with neither beginning nor ending, only "now."

In this bonding, Nature holds the links of change. Just as Nature continually changes all within her realms — physically and metaphysically — so also Nature changes mankind.

There are times when this change is slow, gradual, and subtle. At other times giant leaps are experienced, with all the accompanying shock and trauma.

Prepare for a giant leap, but take comfort, for despite how it appears, such leaps are always forward.

I must admit that when I had approached the Cycad seedlings in the bush-house, my mind was caught in reflection and speculation on the past, but now the intensity of energy moving through me spiraled around and around the powerful words which claimed my attention: "Prepare for a giant leap." The past once again formed an association with the present as memories of boyhood unfolded in my mind's eye.

I WAS TEN YEARS OLD when Granchester was flooded. How well I remember my father driving his beloved Austin Ten gently into the floodwater on the road near Byron's Pool, and the thrill of washing the car and soaking my brother under such extraordinary circumstances. The floodwaters receded, leaving Byron's Pool Woods muddy, smelly, and dirty from the rampaging water. With three other boys, I remember picking over the debris, exploring the changes wrought by the water's power when our wanderings brought us to the Gully.

Today I realize that the Gully was no more than a small stream cutting at an angle into the woods, joining the river further downstream. With the advent of time, the stream eroded a passage through a ridge in the woods, gradually cutting a gully about three yards deep. The water was always cold, shallow, and shaded, but the large colorful Minnows flashed electric tones of red and blue in the clear, sparkling water.

Despite the receding floodwaters, water gushed in a brown and dirty torrent along the Gully, but to our surprise the bank was cut wider, the Gully deeper, by more than a yard. Adventure beckoned, danger adding the required thrill of daring. Gazing at the Gully, speculation soon developed about the new width. Was it still jumpable?

"Of course it is." Lennie made the statement with scorn. Even in his early years he had his father's barrel chest and strong build, and looking at him the rest of us had no doubt that he could jump it. Terry walked to the Gully edge, peering into the foaming rush of water.

"I can jump it."

Another statement of fact. Terry was the dedicated athlete,

excelling in all sports, superior to the others in our gang when physical expertise was required.

Eddie crowed loud his ability, "Yeh! Anyone could jump this." And with his long, lanky legs, who could doubt it?

All eyes fixed on me. Walking to the Gully I peered into the dirty water and across to the other side. Golly, it sure had moved back a ways!

"No problem," I said. "It isn't all that wide." A lie to my inner feelings of doubt.

We turned away and paced back for a comfortable run; the jumping began. First went Eddie. Long legs pumping, he soared over, as expected, clearing it easily. Lennie and Terry followed in quick succession, both leaping the Gully. I made my run and, gathering myself for the jump, slithered to a stop on the very edge of the bank, tottering to regain balance. A moment's silence . . . an inbreath, and then the jeering started. Embarrassed, my face flaming red, I turned about, once more facing the jump, and again ran hard at the Gully—to again abort the leap. A third attempt, the same result. I endured the remainder of the day, thankful when we got home and I could no longer hear the snide remarks, the hidden sneers.

I lay awake that night for hours, tormented by the jump I had failed. School next day was bearable because Eddie, Lennie, and Terry went to a different school, so nobody knew of my failure. Cycling home I took an alternative route, taking me through Granchester and past Byron's Pool Woods. Leaving my bike in the Hawthorn hedge at the entrance gate, I walked into the Woods to the Gully.

I stood on the Gully edge, poised—preparing for a giant leap forward. Standing quiet, no longer responding to taunts and pressure, I realized I had no fear of the actual jump, yet fear lurked vague and disturbing in the background. I stared into the dirty water, changed by the swirling mud to menacing depths. This was the problem. I needed to see into the water, to see clearly, to see my way ahead. If I fell, I needed to know what awaited, but with the water brown and murky an element of the unknown crept in, subtle, but devastating to my morale. With recognition of my failing I turned around, paced a short run, and facing the Gully, I ran to take the leap — and failed — and failed — and failed — and failed — and failed — and SUCCEEDED!

On the sixth attempt I soared high over the Gully, landing a yard clear on the other side. The feeling which swept over me was incredible. I had jumped far more than a gully. The Gully was symbolic; I had jumped the unknown. All my life I have been facing giant leaps forward, hurdling yet other unknown factors. And now, from the intelligence of an ancient palm, the leap was brought forward once more. Never had I faced such an "unknown" as I now faced, no longer a physical jump, but a leap in consciousness. Another leap across the eroding gully of my own fear — the fear of the unknown.

FOLLOWING OUR MOVE to where we now live, our daughter Tracy insisted that because we had more room we must have a Christmas tree. After several years cramped in various caravans, we all agreed with her, so one particular day found me searching for a suitable candidate.

We have a couple of towering Hoop Pines on the property, and I figured that finding a small tree would not be difficult. A walk in the bush revealed several small trees, but always a tentative inquiry brought forth a strong objection to being moved into a pot. Empty-handed, I wandered back to the huge Morton Bay Fig tree and there, close to the trunk, a one-yard-high Hoop Pine was struggling to establish itself. Ah ha, I thought, this tree has no future at all with its close proximity to the big fig, so this will be our Christmas tree. Although a fraction underdeveloped on one side, the tree was perfect for our needs. The decision was made and, willing or not, this would be the tree. An inquiry found the Pine very willing, so I began the task of excavation.

From the beginning it was a calamity. I followed the main tap root for no more than the length of my hand when it vanished under an enormous fig tree root. Laying down my spade, I directed my thoughts to the Pine. "I'm sorry, but I shall have to chop through your root. Almost certainly it will kill you. To give you a chance I suggest you withdraw your energy from your roots, and tomorrow I will remove you and replant you in a large pot."

Next day on the site, with a suitable container, I severed the root and the Pine came away. Looking rather pathetic with only one short root stump and a single wisp of side root, the tree was set into its pot and firmed down. Only hours elapsed before the Pine was drooping at its growing tip. To make it look more presentable for decorations, I twisted some thin, malleable wire around and up the prickly stem to support it. The children decorated the tree, and on Christmas day it looked quite splendid receiving admiration, love, and thanks for its part in our festivities.

Following New Year's day the Pine was placed outdoors in a shady spot and received regular water. I waited for it to die before I abandoned it, for, despite the water, there were no roots to receive the life-giving moisture. Six months later I carefully unwound the wire from a vigorous, sturdy tree delighting at being in the pot and ready for the Christmas ahead. It was mid-November, six weeks before the day, when I felt drawn toward a deeper attunement.

"Tell me, did the other Hoop Pines refuse to become our Christmas tree because you needed moving, or did you as a par-ticular tree wish to be more involved with us? Also, how did you survive the transplanting which was little short of brutal?"

I looked at the Pine, silent and motionless, while doubt reopened old wounds in my mind.

Relax, my friend. Do not be drawn into old thought pat-terns; relax in this new movement. Doubt is an established pattern of confusion which will deny your experience. Relax. To answer your question I would ask you to discard the physical aspects of transplanting a tree. I am not separate in conscious-ness from each separate physical tree you wished to take. Each tree can be likened to an aspect of "one" consciousness. Within this is your challenge. Your science has made great inroads in the study of plants and physical life forms, but in the more subtle regions of life—energy—consciousness so very little has been realized or recognized.

This is why your choice was made, for I as a Tree could demonstrate your own power of love. My long root was destroyed, my connection with the earth and its elements erased. Yet in the time lapse when you suggested I withdraw my energy, it was withdrawn on nonphysical levels of which your science knows nothing. Had I received ingratitude, indifference, or neglect, I would have quickly died, for my energy reserve was, and is, united with your own spiritual energy.

The inner light—power—which is your family became a socket into which I could plug for energy. You and your family sustained me. Thus fed, I had the energy to grow a new root system.

I paused and reread the words which had flowed so easily from the Silence into my mind. I tried not to question the truth and wisdom of life, but it crossed my mind that to prove my experience was close to impossible. The thought was picked up immediately.

Proof has become mankind's obsession. It is an intellectual attachment which, rather than expanding your horizons, is rapidly becoming a restriction. Proof can easily become a denial of that which "IS," and the seed of tragedy are contained in this. Those who feel these words resonate in their hearts will need no proof, while those who do not could accept none.

Just as you will never physically witness my maturity as an individual tree, neither must you seek to witness the maturity of seed you sow in the hearts of those who seek to understand. Remain open and relaxed. I stand close to you each day, and our growth is combined. Seek more often to unite your spiritual energy with that of our kingdom.

Let us communicate often, that we both may benefit.

Between the Christmas tree's outdoor position and the Cycad Palms, we have a Crepe Myrtle – a large deciduous shrub with spectacular red flowers in the summer. This particular Myrtle is host to a range of epiphytes, mostly Staghorn and Elkhorn Ferns. The host is considerate, offering sun and light in the cooler winter months, with mottled shade and protection in the hot summer months.

One of the plants enjoying this hospitality is a species I much admire. It has many names: Old Moss Beard, Solomon's Beard, Long Moss, but I think Spanish Moss is the most common – and misleading. The true name is Tillandsia. A member of the Bromeliad family, it is epiphytic, hanging in long silver-gray streamers from the trees of tropical America. Rather like a tufted, gray, open moss, it is, in fact, a series of tiny, interlaced plantlets needing no roots and feeding on the airborne nutrients contained in the continuous moisture of its natural regions. It is easily grown in a warm climate or in a glasshouse; although not attractive to everyone's taste, it has great appeal to me. We grow Spanish Moss using an old pine cone as both anchor and natural moisture meter. The pine cone opens wide when dry, but kept damp to the plant's liking remains firmly closed. With our mild climate, it hangs in a tree outdoors, but I keep it in full view so we can appreciate its delicate beauty. I assumed our Spanish Moss was happy with this arrangement, but one day I decided to ask it. "Does your location suit you, Spanish Moss, and do you find it pleasing to receive our admiration?" In my subtle awareness I could feel the energy of this plant magnifying – an energy of far greater proportion than the small tuft before me.

I feel it a privilege you have chosen our energy to be involved in the lesson of synthesis which you have undertaken.

The words, silent but with power, invoked an instant recollection of how I bought this plant from a shop in Sydney. I remembered my delight when I found it in a flower shop. Silly as it seems, it is the only recollection I have of that particular visit to Sydney.

When a person feels as strongly as you about a plant we cannot help but be affected. Today you learned why this is so. You hold the privilege of conscious unity according to your will. We welcome this contact and will do all in our power to further the experience.

During my early morning meditation I was shown a physical view of my connection with the plant kingdom when we communicate. I was standing in a clearing in a light, open forest. I was being guided and instructed by something I knew as the Spirit of the Forest.

Look now at your hands, your body.

Holding my hands before me, I was able to see light radiating from them. It was rather like an aura, but of a quite different energy. I could perceive this light radiating from my whole Being.

See now the tree directly before you.

The nearest tree was about twenty yards from me. With magnificent dark foliage, it was a tree of a variety unknown to me. However, like me, the tree radiated light, swirling and moving around its trunk and leaves, governed by an unseen power.

Reach out to the tree with your awareness. Direct your consciousness to the tree, embracing it with love.

Even as I probed with inquiry out to the tree, light leapt from my body, my Being, and in a microsecond embraced the tree, uniting and combining with the light energy of the tree. In the linking, I felt the surging Intelligence of Nature welcoming the bond.

This demonstrates clearly the spiritual union which takes place. Each time you project your conscious awareness to a plant or any aspect of Nature's kingdom, thus does your radiance leap forth. Neither distance nor time may dispel this union. We have enabled you to witness this truth, that you may more easily cast aside your doubt. Doubt within certain limits can

*be of value, but when doubt becomes focused and maintained
by habit, it may destroy the radiance you have witnessed.*
Let your perception widen . . . and understand.

No longer was I united with a tree, but with the whole
forest, "one" radiant light. My perception rose above the forest
where I witnessed the collective radiance composed of countless
individual lights, united and fused into a single glowing radiance. Higher, far above the forest, an even greater radiance shone
forth . . . and on . . . out and out . . . in and in . . . until, beyond
vision or perception, I knew all light converged into a single
celestial brilliance.

Now, standing on the lawn beneath its host tree, I was able
to look at the Spanish Moss hanging before me, comfortable
with the space between us, knowing the connection.

*Within our blended consciousness, radiance communi-
cates. Your thoughts are known, and likewise, as you become
more receptive, you will "know" us.*

*Like bubbles floating to the surface of a pond, so will
awareness trickle from your higher conscious Self. Always you
must seek "knowing" rather than knowledge, for this is your
chosen path. In "knowing," our energy, far more than is at present conveyed, will become realized. Knowing is realized knowledge, the living word. "Knowing" is timeless and spaceless,
bound by no laws.*

My mind gave an immediate demonstration of its fickle-
ness as a thought hit me.

"Tell me, so often one plant follows on from another with a
line of ideas or concepts. Is this deliberate?"

The Spanish Moss waved daintily in the breeze.

*The only reason for this is you. Just as your inner radiance
projects you—the real "you"—into the kingdom of Nature, so
it projects your strengths, weaknesses, and needs.*

Thus, although there may be disparity in your questions,

the root cause remains fairly constant. In meeting your needs it is not unnatural that one experience overlaps, extends from, or converges with another set in the apparent past.

My head spun with the sudden deepening of images and concepts. I decided to give it a rest.

Tomorrow is another day . . . I think!

4
December

I<small>T CONCERNS ME</small> that the human race has allowed separation
from Nature to become established as accepted reality.
Hence, man and Nature, rather than man of Nature. A mid-
century edition of *Chamber's Dictionary* defines Nature in a
very appropriate way as the power which creates and regulates
the world. I find this definition most acceptable. Dimensions of
grandeur, power, and timelessness are conjured up in the imagination, yet it also poses a question. Do we as humanity stand
above and beyond such power, or is such a concept so far beyond
us that we are forever lost to such reality? Observation would
seem to indicate that mankind is a facet of Nature, hopefully a
roving, latent intelligence. I use the word "latent" with delibera-
tion. Regretfully, our continual involvement in the violence of
war, our ever-increasing environmental pollution, as well as the
expanding proportion of mentally-stressed people in our society
clearly demonstrate that "intelligence" is not at the forefront of
human endeavor. At best, a greed-oriented intellectual arrogance
is evident. Thank God, however, the normal, everyday folk, in
times of crisis, draw upon the highest qualities we have within
us. However, this is no longer enough. "We" are the Nature we
abuse. To establish a reconnection with Nature is to reach into
our Selves, reconnecting with the timeless wisdom we each con-

tain. Few people are not presented with opportunities to reestablish their connection with Nature, but few indeed are the people
who will allow themselves time for this process. We are hyped-
up whirlwinds heading blindly nowhere. How—where—when
does it end? Do we take responsibility for ourselves, or do we
invest our power in the mythical "they" who we believe created
the mess we are in?

I have learned that this "connection" with Nature tran-
scends the physical connection, becoming an involvement with
the Spirit. Seemingly we are required to stand alone, humble and
vulnerable before the Spirit of Nature, which paradoxically
is the Spirit of Self. We are no longer required to relate to humanity "and" Nature, but rather humanity "as" Nature. Within
this framework there develops a union, one of joy, a joy rising
triumphant over all outside stress, making the moment whole
and complete.

ONE SUNNY MORNING Treenie and I were sitting with our
friend Yvonne, chatting in her living room. The room
was light and fern filled. The full length of one side was
glass from floor to ceiling and afforded superb views of the
nearby rainforest sweeping as a green carpet up the escarpment
to the New England Plateau. An atmosphere of intimacy with
Nature was invoked. Sweet-scented climbers and soft-leaved
shrubs waited, ever ready to clamber inside, knocking with gentle persistence in the light breezes sneaking from the forest. Our
conversation was interesting and intense, but my attention was
distracted by a small, variegated Jade plant growing in a clay pot
outside the window. The wide veranda housed a motley collec-
tion of miscellaneous plants which were generally required to
survive by their own hardiness. Indoors was a different story; the
many ferns responded to the care and attention they received. I
recognized the Jade; I had given it to Yvonne when we left the
area two years earlier. It had not grown. The pot was large
enough to allow for growth, but the Jade languished—it was
stunted, but tenacious and alive.

"How would you like to be a Bonsai?" I silently asked.
The Jade's energy perked up immediately.

That would be most acceptable. In form I am Bonsai already.

I looked at Yvonne, smiling innocently.
"Do you want the little variegated plant out there?" I asked her.
"Do you?"
Yvonne is nothing if not direct. I knew that any "ers" or "ums" were useless. Clarity and honesty were required.
"Yes, I do. I would like to Bonsai it," I responded.
"It's yours," Yvonne replied.
So that was that.
I looked again at the Jade — stunted, twisted, almost grotesque. Strange, but when previously I thought of Jade as a Bonsai subject it had felt wrong. This felt right.
Next day I decided to pursue the matter further with the variegated Jade. It seems repetitive, but Jade is another favorite. There is a quality to the Jade energy which triggers a response in me, a surge of recognition, a feeling of "something else." I placed the little, stunted plant at my side, asking the question uppermost in my mind. "Why have you not grown? Despite looking stunted you feel quite different. What is this 'difference'?"

Are you ready to stretch some more?

I sighed. "What now? Oh well, why not?"

This moment is/has been known. I have waited for this to happen. I grew as I needed to grow. Is it not true that had I been well grown, a perfect specimen, you would have been uninterested?

I felt baffled — yes, it was true.

Space-time is convoluted. It exists not, yet it exists. Time is relative to your experience. To your physical world, time marches on. Time in inner reaches is nonexistent. Will be . . . is . . . has been are all one. Different places in the same cycle of

Now. The moment of you receiving me the second time was known before I even began to grow as the cutting which you once removed.

Follow it back further.

When you removed me as a cutting from the large parent plant, even the particular cutting was known, chosen before you knew the plant existed or even had a thought of taking a Jade cutting. So it proceeds—back and back—forward and forward—all connected—no random incidents—no chances— all choice—within no choice at all.

"Whoa—hang on a bit. Of choice within no choice, I am familiar. But applying that to such a mundane act as taking a cutting of a Jade four years ago, that's ridiculous."

My outburst was indignant, but the Jade continued as though uninterrupted.

Always a higher truth is in expression. A far greater Intelligence than that which mankind calls intelligence maintains order within a world of apparent chaos.

Man claims intelligence as a thought process, whereas in truth he measures only intellect. Intelligence makes no mistakes, there are none to be made. Even the apparent threat of mankind to the stability of your planet is no more than a movement within an uncomprehended dream.

No . . . not even the choice of a cutting from a forgotten Jade in the remote stretches of Australia is chance, or accident. I have grown as I have grown. I have followed the pattern of growth which is perfect for me.

Intelligence "IS."

Intelligence decides who or what shall follow a pattern of deformity, a travesty of that which you would call perfect. Even though the physical form may be flawed, or crippled, there is no mistake, for in the infinite pursuit of truth, of expansion, of balance, a gift is contained within such adversity, a gift most rare, yet hidden.

Accept a humble, twisted Jade. My "difference" is my perfection. See your own belief and thought process in a similar fashion, knowing that your experience is but a different angle of the "One" mirror.

We will grow together for as long as is necessary, whether that is to end this moment or many years hence. It will be not chance, but choice.

It will be not physical, but spiritual.

The energy quieted, the silent words stilled. I sat for a while in a contemplative mood. For the previous few days I had felt threatened. I questioned if this experience of mine of listening to and talking with the plants was real or imagined. I dialogued with Treenie, asking not for answers — I did not know the questions — but for honesty, hoping her insight might reveal my oversight. I had visited Yvonne with a vague hope that dialogue could help expose the hidden threat as seen from her different perspective; instead . . . I came home with the Jade.

Maybe that was it. I felt a sense of excitement. Maybe the Jade was my answer. An answer offered four years before I knew the question. Maybe . . . if . . . but . . . my mind reeled at the sudden onslaught of concepts. One surprising fact emerged: I could accept the words of the Jade, despite their being thrown with full Jade vigor. I felt okay. The threat had faded. I pondered. What had changed? Why could I accept in this moment, while retreating in confusion and fear in another? The inner voice came clearly once again.

Truth is as a wave upon the beach. It races high, smothering the sand with its energy, and the sand knows the wave. The tide recedes. The sand is dry, and it knows not the wave or even its source. With the noonday sun, doubt is high upon it . . . until again comes the nourishing waves of truth.

Thus in your heart do the tides of truth and doubt ebb and flow. Be not concerned by this, for in mankind this is as natural as the waves upon a beach.

Know your Self as a single grain on the beach of humanity. You can choose to become saturated in the waves of truth, or, as others do, you can choose to let truth drain from you, unable to penetrate the hard shell of indifference.

*You may control—for your Self only—the ebb and flow.
You can remember the salt tang of truth when the tide recedes,
and, in remembering, truth will for all time be "known."*

I looked at my stunted, twisted Jade. A respect I had never
before felt moved within me. As if a veil had lifted, I saw the
Jade anew.

THE SUN BEAT DOWN from a cloudless sky; it was another
very hot day. For a week we had unremitting heat,
unusually so for our valley, and each afternoon the cool
river became our refuge. One afternoon when the heat was reaching its peak, I was again heading through the garden, river bound.

Please pick my bloom and take me from this heat.

I stopped, suddenly aware of the roses in their bed of mulch,
and of a single red Rose which had burst from bud to full bloom.
The heat was too much for the flower, rather than the plant, and
I marvelled that the plant should wish to protect its single precious flower. Fetching the shears, I cut the Rose and placed it in
a slim, water-filled vase at a focal point in our living room. The
air was considerably cooler, and the fragrance of the red Rose
blended happily with the atmosphere.

Several days later the heat intensified rather than abated,
and even the living room became uncomfortably hot by late
afternoon. The Rose, which under cooler conditions would still
be fresh, was dying, each petal darkening at the tips from the
stress of heat. I extended my conscious love to the fading Rose,
moved by its beauty despite its plight.

"Thank you, fading Rose. Thank you for sharing your
beauty and fragrance with us. I only wish we could have sustained you longer."

*Do not mourn a dying Rose. I die, yet I live, for am I not
also the Rose in the garden, all Roses in all gardens, all Roses in
all vases? My petals have dried out, but if it were not for the*

love I have felt from you I would have collapsed the first day. See, not a petal has fallen.

The energy of those who love our kingdom carries within it a nourishment. Thus you have nourished me. I sing a song of fading radiance, yet it is within this unseen radiance I live. Physical death is of little concern. Death is our constant companion, accompanying each moment, yet death is meaningless. Death implies— "without life"—but this is untrue. Only the form, the physical shell, may be surrendered.

Life is infinite, ever present, ever expanding.

In the radiance of my flower, I live. In the radiance of your Being, I live forever.

Our energies are blended and in you I am whole.

The silent voice faded, but while I looked again at the Rose, I felt its energies gathering. I had felt uneasy with the content of images and words from this Rose; perhaps I was moved out of my depth, but the Rose sensed my distress.

Do not force your mind to accept our truth in your crystallized concepts. Be free, be open. Allow my words to move through you freely and easily.

Nothing must be seized and held. Do not make knowledge of my words. Let the ideas be vague and shifting, sifting and sorting their own energy, presenting, with the perfect timing of acceptance, a higher truth.

I can never die, even as a flower, for I am of you. Such a statement challenges you. Immediately—despite my suggestion—your mind seeks to grasp and understand.

My friend, let the heart know truth which the mind cannot yet comprehend. Explanations become useless. Cast aside knowledge based only on a physical reality. You must become attuned to another world, a dimension within and without your own dimension.

Let your heart accept, even while the mind paces in its cage of outraged belief.

When you learn of a physical truth, you accept and believe because you can see it. Do not deny a simultaneous truth vibrating to a higher wisdom simply because it may not be seen.

Place your faith in "knowing." Trust your Self. I will say no more — I sense your stress.

Remember, love is the bond, and love is the release.

I found it very demanding to have images and ideas, thoughts, feelings, and words pouring into me which had no easy lodging place. They did not fit. Often I feel as though I am standing alone on a tiny island. The island is my known and accepted belief, that which is real to everyone. Gradually my island is being washed away as wave after wave of the unknown, the "not evident," erodes the sand from beneath my feet. I feel that our accepted truths are as firm as sand. It is as though I must step onto the rock of a higher truth, knowing that, once secure, I must step again to a different rock governed by a different set of rules. Only now am I beginning to realize that casting myself into unknown waters, in trust, is the most difficult act I have ever undertaken. But I am inspired to persist.

T HE HEAT HAD FINALLY BROKEN. Clouds gathering during the day passed slowly and heavily over the valley. Rain was threatening when I reached the river, not to swim in the water, but to immerse myself in the waiting consciousness. I sat with open journal on my lap, my mind reaching out to the river. With the flow of words came a simultaneous scattering of rain, sweeping in from upriver.

Your anticipation, loaded with expectation, dampens our communication in much the same way as the rain dampens your ability to write.

My pen, moving over the paper surface, was forming half words, part sentences. Where it was wet, nothing I wrote would impress on the paper.

Thus, my friend, when you try to attune with anticipation

and expectation, we find you as the wet pages of your journal, only capable of receiving a fraction of what we wish to convey.

I recoiled in dismay.

A glimpse of my subconscious expectations was revealed in the clouded mirror of self-reflection. Dejected, I walked heavily back to the house, rain sweeping over me. Dropping the journal on my desk, I sat down thoughtfully. How could I deal with thoughts I was not aware of thinking? It was a ridiculous problem. Which came first, the chicken or the egg? If expectation is based on thought, or anticipation is unconscious activity of the mind, how can I break into this cycle? Glancing through the window I noticed the rain had stopped. For some reason it seemed to be a vaguely mocking gesture, as though Nature scorned my attempts to successfully capture her wisdom on paper. With incredible sincerity, the silent words of river entered my confused and whirling mind.

We do not mock you. Indeed, you are privileged that life offered such a perfect reflection of your expectations. Your subconscious rumblings cause a disturbance in the flow between us. You are as yet unaware of the power of thought. Directed and focused, thought is of immense power. Suppressed and unconscious thoughts or desires cause a distortion in the clarity we seek to impart.

A subconscious pattern of thought is an interruption between us. Before you are ready to use the full power of focused thought, it must become clear, pure, and refined.

Cluttered, imprisoned, and suppressed thought is a danger, seeking always to hold the thinker in bondage. Thought should not be imprisoned. Look into the dungeon of your mind and release any locked-up thoughts. Let them go free. Attach no claim on them. Be not embarrassed by them, simply release them.

To do this you must acknowledge the thoughts which shame you, accept their existence. Speak them aloud to a loving friend, or into the Silence. In the speaking they shall be released, no longer holding you by their unspoken deceit.

*In the release of these thoughts, you shall find your own
release. Only by the release of thoughts as they arise into the
conscious mind shall you master thought.*

The dialogue left me feeling bemused and rather disturbed.
I was still feeling a sense of shock. I had been unaware of expectations, the imprisoned manipulations; yet, in honesty, I was
aware of the shadows which flitted to and fro deep in the mind. I
wanted no prisoners in the cells of my mind, but I was not sure I
could release them or what would happen if I tried.

Day met and merged with night, but the following morning
a cloud weighed heavily over me, anchored by a subconscious
attachment to bygone fears. I realized that a past laden with
unresolved problems is ever present and continually represented
until we develop the capacity to resolve our problems. By this
action we lay the past to rest.

Thoughts slid through my mind with deceptive ease as,
squinting against the glare of the early, low sun, I gazed at the
nearby Rubber tree.

If only doubt would never plague my mind again. Despite
thoughts of pessimism, I could feel the consciousness of the tree
becoming alive and aware in my mind. If only I could be at peace
with my knowing.

I am sorry, my friend, truly sorry.

*We can offer you no proof. What do you need? Would a
recorded communication heard simultaneously by a dozen or
even a thousand people meet your need?*

*Or would you then be one of a small group of confused and
victimized people seeking further proof? Only by knowing who
you are will you find peace. When this is known, proof will be
revealed as an offering needed only by those who cannot accept
the reality of their own lives.*

*Doubt holds you away from your acceptance of Self. I need
not tell you that doubt is a lock on the door to greater realities,
to extended possibilities. Doubt is the part of your mind which*

fights to retain control. Doubt seeks to speculate and, from speculation, to walk a known path.

You cannot do this and enter a higher conscious awareness. There is no room for doubt, no place for doubt to express its fear. Doubt destroys faith. Faith knows not, nor seeks to know, for in faith this moment is complete.

The path of faith is a journey beyond time, space, or dimensional limitations.

The mind may not go ahead seeking to make the way known. Instead, the mind is controlled, neither by leash nor techniques, but by the faith of this moment's "knowing."

Please understand. Known is the past, while "knowing" is only of this moment, the eternal "now."

Can you accept a challenge of this magnitude?

Can you leave the company of the vast flock of those who doubt, to become a lonely shepherd of faith?

A feeling of unease swept me, not so much related to doubt, but to a vague inner disturbance I could not identify. I decided to be gentle with myself rather than glare within, seeking to expose the lurking feelings and drag them into a premature light. I was aware of the conscious friendship of this tree, of Nature.

"Thank you," I murmured, "thank you."

The silent word took me by surprise.

Be aware of how much more easily you are now accepting the presence of a higher truth. No longer do you fight for weeks and months against the loaded logic of doubt.

Be content to accept for now the presence of higher truth. It will fit in your consciousness, involving and enveloping you with perfect timing.

Yes. I felt that it was true. Doubt no longer fought me for week after pain-filled week. Doubt was still a fierce predator, but a crippled one, no longer able to rend and tear at my faith, yet ever lurking, snarling its menace from the background. A sense of gratitude swept over me, for I know I have been helped, almost nursed, through the last year.

My mind flickered through the recorded events. A year of pain, of confrontation and decision. Either I walked my long long-ago-chosen path, or I turned aside completely. It was my choice.

To hesitate in confusion and doubt was to sink deeper into stagnation and despair.

I sighed. "I am so glad the worst is behind me, the decision made."

It is good that you are aware of the help which has been extended to you. One day you will know how your pain was our pain; your confusion, our compassion; your doubt, our sorrow.

We have extended our kingdom to you to seal a bond, to allow a commitment to grow, to mature into flower, and to send forth the seed of its fruit. We shall meet on the other levels one day. We shall meet in a radiance of such light that truth shall forever stand revealed.

For several days a strange, disoriented feeling pervaded me. I felt as though a deep, inner part had made a giant step, while the other part neither knew where nor how to make such a move.

I felt off balance, an inner disturbance. The inevitable happened. I began to develop a cold, starting with a typical sore throat.

That was yesterday.

Today it was nicely developed. My glands were swollen, my sinuses were blocked, and a mild headache throbbed behind my eyes. Now I had an excuse to hide, to linger a while in self-pity. There is nothing quite like a cold or flu to avoid an issue!

At my request, Treenie went to the pharmacy as soon as it opened and returned home with a packet of throat lozenges which she flipped onto the bed with a remarkable lack of sympathy.

It was while she was away "something happened."

I had been reading *Illusions* by Richard Bach for the second time, maybe two years after my first reading. The book poses questions. Where is the boundary between reality and illusion? Who decides what is real and what is illusion? Do we accept a common belief, or can we have an independent belief, isolated, but real? How much of our experience is an illusion based on what we think or expect is reality?

I have seen a man stick a long pin right through his arm. No tricks, the genuine article. He obviously felt no pain. He was not in a trance. He taught himself that it is possible to shift his identity away from his arm or any other part of his body; thus, he felt no pain in an arm that was not his. Stick the pin through my arm and . . . PAIN. Who has the correct reality? Who lives in illusion?

I know which I prefer. I browsed over the concept of limitation. We are limited by the conditioning of our thoughts, by what we think we can achieve, by what we think will gain the approval of our peers, thus stabilizing our self-esteem – another illusion. On and on . . . .

Struggling through this long, murky turmoil of thought, a light appeared, drawing swiftly closer, flooding my mind with illumination. Something clicked . . . a giant stride . . . .

If this is an illusion I am experiencing with Nature, if it is all imagination – then it's okay. I like it. Who can make me a better offer? Polluted food and air? Is that better? To maintain a belief in death, fear, greed? Are they better? A dogmatic religion with a judgmental God? Is that better? My experience is uplifting, expanding, loving, creative, intelligent. Who can offer me a better reality or illusion? If I feel a great love toward Nature, and I feel love radiating to me from Nature, who has a better illusion to offer? If I feel compassion and love for humanity, if I am happy doing exactly what I want to do, who can offer me more than this?

Suddenly it hit me. What am I fighting? Am I fighting an offer of love, of peace, of expansion, of creativity, of insight and intelligence, of knowing "me," of what "IS"? Fighting it for what? Do I want to remain with the common belief of pain, suffering, death, drudgery, sickness, of being the victim of life's misfortune – when I know I can be who I am, where I am, when I am? Right . . . "now."

When Treenie flipped the throat lozenges onto my bed, I

took one . . . and I "knew." I am not denying the pain, fear, doubt, sorrow of everyday reality, but neither need I cling to such a powerful belief while denying the creative, intelligent love of Nature. I chose that, for me, pain and suffering, fear and doubt were ended. We all have that choice. I don't want a cold or sore throat. I don't need a cold or sore throat. I've done it all before. I no longer need to. I am free. I accept my experience. I believe my experience. I know what I know. I can offer my gift to enrich life through the pages of my books, but it does not matter how many or how few want it. I do. I enjoy it. I scrambled out of bed, a feeling of excitement upon me. I knew it was a breakthrough. To where, I had no clue, but the step was enough. To make it public and thus become vulnerable, I told Treenie and the family I would not have a sore throat and cold, sharing with them something of what had taken place. They greeted most of my words with suppressed smirks and a "we will see" expression.

Now, at the end of the day as I sit with Jade, writing and relating this magnificent plant energy, I have no sore throat or cold. It took about thirty minutes for all the symptoms to completely disappear. I like it!

THE SMALL DARK-BLUE BONSAI POT was the perfect container. I felt a sense of achievement as I gazed at the Jade, one long root thrown carelessly over a small boulder, growing as though no other pot had ever contained it. The Jade and I had combined consciously, finding the most perfect way in which to express our synthesis. The stunted, twisted form, ugly in its previous container, became pure beauty. It is almost too perfect.

I directed my thoughts to the Jade. Jade would listen, Jade would understand.

Do you feel our song of triumph? Do you feel the cosmic All surging through your Being? We rejoice with you, my friend. You are taking the steps which will gain you mastery of your destiny, rather than becoming flotsam cast high on the beach of helplessness, at the mercy of all who pass by. Now do you understand our union? Time between time ceases to be. I sing in your heart, for you are my creator.

Stretch again and comprehend. It was you who created me, that I may tell you . . . you are creator. You of humanity.

By your will, by your thoughts, by your imagination, by your belief, you make it so.

There is that in you which knows.

In all mankind there is that which knows.

Life is not revealed by building up layer upon layer of stored information.

This becomes knowledge. Knowledge is information made static. Life is revealed by "knowing."

"Knowing" is information in movement, kept free, spontaneous. Science has a fixation on knowledge, particularly that which is compatible with sense perception.

Despite instruments which far exceed man's sensory capacity, all knowledge gained is translated back to a sense perception before it can be coded as "information."

If it cannot be seen, heard, touched, smelled, or tasted, it is not received by physical man. The five senses of man. The four walls and the lid of your prison. Discard them. Touch will not determine subtle shapes. Eyes will not perceive reality. Ears do not hear the song of the universe. You cannot taste the food of angels or smell the fragrance of a higher truth. We rejoice as you begin to unshackle the self-imposed chains of limitation.

Use your physical senses, enjoy them, but never for one moment believe in them as complete reality. Your heart knows — experience.

Believe, believe.

Whatever you believe — is so.

The feeling of excitement surged. The sore throat, headache, and cold "had" gone. Were they ever a reality, or were they an illusion I created to hide behind? Whichever, I controlled them. I felt excited because I had never done this before. What is illusion? What is real? One thing I know for certain, I don't know where I'm going, but I'm ready to enjoy the journey. Expansion—love—creativity—Nature—knowing. Does anyone have a better offer?

TIME PASSES . . . but the sense of movement, inner movement, has not faded. I feel an inner "aliveness," an awareness more sharp, bright, and clear than ever before. I feel I am poised, balanced and unafraid, on the edge of some mystical insight. In some strange way I know, even though I am not aware of knowing. I have no idea where my connection with Nature will take me, yet I am more committed to the journey than ever. Along this path lies inner fulfillment, and I can linger no more.

No longer is doubt casting gray and melancholy shadows over a sunlit horizon; my step can quicken naturally. Change is an obvious factor in our lives. I see change as never before, strikingly obvious. Now I can trust the process in which I am involved. I can trust who I am, knowing that only the most perfect expression of Nature/Self can result. My acceptance is of my choosing, yet my choice was made long ago. How many of us are destined to honor commitments we once made and to which we are spiritually obligated?

I suspect there is a very great number of such people on the earth at this time, and I suspect that in this era, when those people connect with their purpose in life, the greatest explosion ever known, of change, of human potential, will take place. These were my thoughts and feelings as I wrote in my journal, and before me on a table, in the dark-blue Bonsai pot, was Jade.

The time on which you speculate is predestined.

Predestined not by some all-powerful God, but by humanity. Ponder a simple parable for its profound truth—"As you sow, so shall you reap."

You cannot take a cutting from a Rose and produce Jade

—you cannot sow arrogance and reap humility. Life is of a vast spectrum.

Life cannot be understood if you acknowledge one brief moment in time—a lifetime. Life cannot be understood if you measure experience as the sum total of many lives.

Life is one vast continuum, in and out of physical matter. Without beginning—without end.

A swim in dense conscious expression this day, and into a finer consciousness next day. Each day/life generates balance. Without the higher worlds of consciousness, your physical existence would rapidly become insanity. What is the reason for this? Could it be random incidents? Could it be that all earth life is an accident or chance of space-time?

Or is it possible that humanity has chosen to become the synthesis of life, blending the physical with the psychical? If this is so, could it be possible that Nature stands not away from, or outside of, humanity, but instead reflects humanity, retains humanity, inflects humanity, both physically and psychically? Can speculation confirm an answer, or does it require that you live it, experience it, become the answer by "Being"?

I stared at the Jade. Wow! Some Jade!

"How do you know all this?" I asked.

Why ask a question when you already know the answer? Do you wish to play more games? Are you not yet ready to accept "knowing"?

"Okay, okay. I accept. I know how you know. Life is one vast universal Intelligence. The life in Nature, the life in humanity, one life, one Intelligence. If you know, I know. We all know. Knowing 'IS.' Life 'IS.' But we of humanity have so much to unknow, unlearn, peel away. Disbelief, doubt, restricted realities, hypnotic limits, an endless list of misbeliefs and conditioned thinking is with us and we have to cope with this. You do not."

I threw my words out almost as a challenge. How incongruous. On glancing at the Jade I realized the incredible physical differences. I could crush it underfoot, no challenge at all, but on inner levels Jade looms so vast I could climb it, rather like a mountain of consciousness from which I could peer ahead. I chuckled. There I go again, why peer ahead? I am here—now. It is enough.

Your words are true about your limitations, even if they are self-imposed and therefore not real. Within our kingdom, light shines with undiminished purity, ever beckoning, ever present.

Such illumination reveals to us our place in the design of life—now. For mankind, however, a greater truth emerges. You are born as creators. Gods of forgotten power. Leaves fallen from a tree to which you know not you belong.

You seek to develop that which "is" developed.

You seek to discover that which "is" discovered. You seek to form in the material world that which you can "know" into being. You seek to prop up your illusions, that you can more easily believe in them. You develop your weaknesses, thus denying the path of inherent strength . . . . Yet we are One . . . and my love envelops you . . . .

The last words caught me off balance. Love became tangible as the words eased with infinite gentleness into my mind. There was a softening of energy, combined with love so overwhelming, so powerful, I glanced around half expecting to find a Spirit of Nature materialized in the room. But no. All I could see was a dark-blue Bonsai pot—and the Jade.

CHRISTMAS ARRIVED, bringing a return of the family. Duncan came from Sydney, exhausted by the frantic pace of life he had designed for himself, and Adrian motorcycled up from Melbourne, bringing a new member into our family, his fiancee, Jo. Once again the Hoop Pine came into the living room and, when draped with the lights and tinsel for celebration, stood forth transformed. I noticed a marked increase in the height, promising the Pine that after one more Christmas it would have the freedom of a garden in which to grow.

Several times during the festivities I sneaked away, seeking attunement with Nature, but each time my mind, overloaded with family involvement, would become lost in the thoughts and speculations of fatherly concern. My mind was hyped-up by the onrush of personalities, the speed, pace, and determination of the kids to extract full measure from the family reunion.

To my consternation I found myself resenting the intrusion, inwardly annoyed that I was isolated from Nature by the demands and pressures of family, but then, taking a good look at myself, I saw the selfishness in such thoughts. This was the family, our children, and here I was resenting their interference in a process which would be waiting with infinite patience until I was ready. Quickly I realized that it was I who was out of step, losing sight of the reality of "now;" and, just as our "grown- up" children needed me, so I needed them for the balance and love which are uniquely human.

I surrendered my isolation by the river to the spontaneity of youth, to the exuberance, energy, and excitement of their holidays.

5
February

THE WEEKS OF JANUARY were swept away by fishing, swimming, talking, laughing, reconnecting with that most precious of human gifts—our own family. The school holidays filled our house with visiting friends, with giggling girls and boisterous boys, each day hurriedly pushing aside the next as the overfilled days sped past in an endless blur of activity.

By the time Duncan, Adrian, and Jo departed I was truly sorry to see them go, feeling again that space inside which, although never empty, is unfilled, lacking the everyday physical relationship of those we love.

Suddenly, abruptly, the holidays were over, the school bus again screeching to a halt outside our gate to pick up Russell and Tracy, our two reluctant scholars. As life slowed down in and around our household, I was able to visit the river with a mind satisfied and enriched by the interactions I had experienced, but now calmed and quiet, reaching out to the Silence of a timeless Nature.

The water was no longer murky with algae as it had been in the warmth of January, for a heavy summer rain had washed and scoured the riverbed clean, each stone fresh-scrubbed and shining, the gravel patches relaid with precise care. Fish were again in evidence, Mullet leaping in a moment's flickering silver, as I crouched over my journal in a mottled patch of shade and light.

It was hot, very hot, the sun relentless in a clear sky. I leapt from the bushes only when the ants launched their third attack. I had been hoping for a truce. The ants, tiny and frenzied in the heat, had driven me from my favorite rock, from the diving board, and now from the shade of the bush.

Finally, I sat rather uncomfortably on the sloping shelf of a large, partly submerged boulder. I felt fairly certain that by sitting in shallow water the ants would be defeated. They were, but two huge March Flies decided I was of great interest to them as they wove in a humming monotone around my head. Waving my hands wildly I shooed them away, not at all keen on their sly, painful bites. The next attack was decidedly sneaky, launched underwater by a crowd of tiddlers and a few large freshwater shrimps. The tiddlers were no problem, but the shrimps — ouch!

I was beginning to feel my timing must be wrong, maybe rivers are just for swimming after all. Though strong in current, the water surface was calm, undisturbed by its swift flow, while shimmering, color-splashed Dragonflies skimmed the water before me, displaying an acrobatic grace surpassing the Swallows flying overhead. A sense of freedom moved into me, expanding and circulating through my awareness.

An effect of sharpening took place, a heightened feeling, one of immense clarity. For a moment I reflected back on old doubts, finally vanquished and beaten. Exhilaration coursed through my body. No longer do I doubt the Intelligence of Nature. No longer do I close my mind to words which flow from the Silence. Silence hides behind that curtain of doubt, hidden by the thick material of physical reality. There was no surging power from the river, nothing on which to focus, but more clearly, more certain than ever, came the silent words.

Silence moves beyond your comprehension.
Listen carefully.

Suddenly, from nowhere, a breeze sprang up, the wind singing again in the needles of the nearby River Oak.

Through all the sound of wind and flute-washed needles; of wind and twisting, chattering leaves; of wind and leaping, splashing Mullet; of wind and gurgling, sighing water; of wind and swaying, dancing trees; another sound too delicate to touch with words pierced me, sweet and poignant, bringing tears unbidden to my eyes.

This "exaltation" played across my senses like a bow moving swiftly over the strings of a violin. Sound which was without, moved within. Sound transcended into Silence, stretching through my consciousness into an infinite wave of tenderness, of clarity and insight. Suddenly, a Mullet leaped with a resounding splash almost under my nose, and the wind ceased. In the Silence all was stilled.

How inadequate your senses are. From your Being, I experienced the Silence of which I am.

How limited, but do not despair.

Only weeks ago even this fleeting experience was quite beyond you, shut away by the self-centeredness which is mankind.

I had to stand up. The agony of pins and needles had turned to cramp, and, easing my nearly dead rear off the rock, I felt a surge of blood rushing into the numbed flesh. I groaned aloud.

"This is how limited I am," I muttered as I paced around, moving my circulation.

"But I get your point about being self-centered. It certainly erases a wider focus on life."

Be gentle with your humanness. It is a privilege to be human, an honor.

Hold in your consciousness the knowing that you—a human—are not limited to bodily experiences. You—a human—may experience the universe, in totality, in Oneness; yet, this experience will not deny a normal identity with the human body. Consciousness will expand, and all will become

*a part of your greater Being. Your identity will be the body of
"earth/man" — humanity — rather than the body of "a man" — a
human. Go now, enjoy the river. I am aware of your discomfort.*

A feeling of something akin to amusement moved into me.
I was aware that "amused" was not the correct descriptive word,
not quite the experience. Maybe the feeling could be described
as an "appreciation" for the lighter aspects of dense reality. I had
the feeling that "I" was the dense reality! Sweating profusely in
the scorching heat, I hopped from foot to foot in an effort to stop
the fierce, biting ants from swarming over my feet. The more I
perspired, the more excited and aggressive they became. It was
time to quit, time to swim.

T HE EXCESS OF FISHING over the school holidays had whet-
ted Russell's appetite for more, and each weekend would
begin with the request: "Can we go fishing, Dad?" Basi-
cally this meant that I was required to act as transport and pack-
horse, for I have little interest in fishing; whereas Russell, with a
fishing rod in his hands, enters a trancelike state of immense
concentration and patience, quite unlike his impatient self at
home.

Perhaps I hedged too often, but Russ decided on a new tac-
tic. He was aware that a friend, John Caporale, had moments of
fishing enthusiasm blowing hot or cold according to the winds
of his desire. With consummate skill, Russ played out a line of
images and fantastic fishing conditions guaranteed to catch any
but the most laggard fisherman.

John succumbed, the hook firmly embedded, and for a few
weekends they visited the local beaches and rivers with varying
degrees of success.

One afternoon I decided to accompany them to the brackish
headwaters of the Bellinger River, an opportunity to observe the
nature of a quite different environment.

Across from where we were sitting on a bank intermingled with stones and grass, the dense vegetation of a Mangrove swamp swept boldly into the water. The water lapping at our feet was clean, yet the depths reflected a brackish-brown, rather like a river of tea flowing impassively to the ocean.

The strident, echoing barks of chained dogs on the nearby dairy farm disturbed a silence fostered and maintained by the softly lapping waves on the rocky shoreline. Crows called harshly from a towering clump of giant Bamboo, while Swallows silently skimmed the water's surface in an endless pursuit of insects. Life was all action, constant motion and movement.

Ten white Egrets flew past, beating their way with visible effort into a head wind, guided by instinct as they winged toward an unknown destination. The tone and pitch of the barking dogs changed abruptly as an evergrowing mob of Friesian cows congregated around the dairy. The daily ritual of milking was about to begin.

My mind drifted . . . way back into my past, to my ten years of milking. It was an old, familiar routine. I felt no envy as the hissing suction of the milking machine began its steady, rhythmic throb, a sound borne faintly on the breeze, yet amplified by ears wise to this particular beat. No! I wanted no part of the past. Necessity had cracked the whip which made me work such long hours at a job I detested, but fear wove the illusion. Fear that my needs could be met by no other way than subservience to a system for which I had no respect. Fear which for a while crowded confidence into a corner, cowering and beaten.

Now I enjoy idle times. Time to feel the empty spaces of this moment. Time to explore the emptiness, the loneliness, to find it full and rich, challenging in the paradox that it takes time to find timelessness.

There came a lull and, except for the keen breeze, activity was suspended. I spoke with the river and the Mangrove swamp, so alien compared with the familiar energy of my river place, with its trees and friendliness. This river felt remote, even though consciously available. Its character, molded by a strange environment, touched my vulnerable emotions with raw indifference.

As wide as I am; as different as I express; as fast as I ebb and flow, yet I am no different from the river with which you communicate. I express another quality, as different as a toe from a finger — and as similar.

The strangeness you feel is your reaction to the environment. It is not river-made or controlled. Your emotions are your response.

Pleasure or displeasure, receptivity or alienation, your choice — or to be more accurate in this instance — your reaction.

In reaction there is no choice.

Learn to be "responsive" rather than reactive, for a world of difference echoes between them.

The wind had increased considerably, blowing cool from the water, but the fishing enthusiasts seemed not to notice. The only thing which they finally did notice was the lack of "response" from the fish they hoped to catch!

M Y VISITS TO OUR RIVER became frequent, inspired and encouraged by the magic energy of the sun. One morning, while sitting on my favorite rock, I gazed upriver to the Weeping Willow tree. The recent flood had left it leaf-bare and stripped. Slender branches shone with a reflection of the palest gold, highlighted by the solid dark-green background of the River Oaks lining the waterway, on and on, upriver.

Bending with supple grace before the violent seasonal winds roaring down the river, or brushing the water's surface in calm tranquility with a touch caressingly light, the Weeping Willow endures all conditions with its nonresistant strength. Flexibility is the quality and essence of Willow. Hemmed in by the vigorous River Oaks massed along the river bank, the Willow stretches far out across the river in its search for sunlight, and it endures. Strong and stalwart as they are, nevertheless, occasional River Oaks are torn from their roothold in every flood, tossed, twisted, and broken in the raging water.

The Willow endures.

It offers no resistance to the rearing strength of pounding floods. Half submerged, the branches writhe and twist, dancing to the river's tune . . . until the flood recedes.

Again the Willow stands free, new leaves quickly replacing the battered foliage. Its strength is masked, yet the Willow makes our finest cricket bats, strong and resilient.

The Willow endures.

The gentlest of river breezes stirred the golden boughs, dancing with a ripple through the tree. The poetry of Nature's finest touch. Appreciation stirred within me. How blessed I am to be surrounded by such beauty, with an even greater blessing: that I allow myself time to experience such golden moments.

We are united in loving awareness.

So enrapt was I in wonder for the beauty manifest before me, that the words moved unexpectedly into my mind.

"I greet you, graceful Willow. I pay my respects to all you represent."

Was it a long-drawn sigh I heard, caught and echoed on a silent breeze?

Respect! Rare indeed is the quality of respect in mankind. To respect each other, to respect Nature—life—requires a respect for Self.

So few, so few indeed, respect their own Selves.

Indeed, the energy we experience most from mankind is Self-loathing buried deep and malignant in the debris of subconscious fear. Small wonder that such loathing, such a lack of Self-respect manifests in sickness, in malignant growths, for such an attitude is a malignancy of the mind.

"How much are you aware of human conditioning? You seem to express insights that we could not possibly credit to a tree."

Your question indicates a slip into old concepts. In the world of Nature to which you attune, a single tree is an illusion. I am "one" with Willow-tree energy. Worldwide, "I am"/"we are" "one" energy. Then again, I am not separate from all tree energy. That which "IS," "Intelligence," "God," "Nature," name it as you desire, this is the power which flows in our sap.

"I am"/"we are" pure Intelligence in our chosen conscious expression and form. You have been told before. Enjoy your five senses, use them wisely to experience your physical dimension, but do not let them deny your psychical expression. Human experience today is limited to the conditioned belief of a renegade mind. Despite appearances, this is neither good nor bad.

It is each person's individual choice.

In the bleakest, most grim personal expression there is "light."

Equally in the most benign and grace-filled person there exists "dark." Balance is the expression of a mature and Self-loved Being. The mind submits to love.

The concept of "nothing is good or bad, thinking makes it so," was not a new one. But I was intrigued by the words "the mind submits to love." There are many seminar experiences available today where we are offered techniques to control the mind, rather as though on a disciplined leash.

"I would like to hear more about the mind and love," I said quietly.

What is there to say? Love is that which "IS."

Before such, the mind submits. He who is controlled by the mind dies to the mind . . . and is reborn.

Such persons relate to the same world, but view it from a different perspective.

They view from Love seeing that which "IS."

Others view from fear seeing that which they believe is.

When others will not support your perception of that which "IS," love will sustain you. When all will support that which is believed in, this maintains the illusion.

It has taken me seven years of conscious inquiry and often painful effort to accept life as I now perceive it, less clouded by my fears.

I am aware fear has not vanished, for, given permission, my mind will quickly conjure up the old images to sustain helplessness.

I had a question.

"Will it take another seven years to reach a state of complete surrender to life, or freedom from all fear?"

Such a question has no answer. You could be love-filled in this moment, transformed in pure "Light," or you could die many years hence screaming your fear. The possibilities exist — your choice.

I have chosen.

Each day life offers me the chance to review my choices. New pressures, lucrative offers, but the price is — to follow a known path.

I cannot do this, yet I am aware these snares hold a gift, for they strengthen my resolve and clarify my sight.

Life offers only upliftment, enlightenment — but as experienced through human sense perception, it is not easy to comprehend or understand. You are aware of the grace of Willow strength. Resilience is strength.

I was aware of a universal law — take that which opposes you, using its strength against itself.

The power is Chi.

Many great men and women have done this.

I stood up, stretching. The Willow appeared unchanged, yet a lightness played around and over the slender branches and leaves. It was not physical. What I could see was different . . . and I knew that I was the difference. Hours passed, while I sat lost in silent contemplation on the old bridge-plank diving board facing upriver.

A gust of wind, sudden and demanding, lifted my head and eyes upriver, and there I saw the voyager.

Exquisitely formed, boat and rider sailed toward me. The boat—a leaf, large and brittle, folded at right angles forming hull and sail.

The rider—a blue Dragonfly, perched daintily in savage splendor atop the sail. The sight of such beauty inspired a poetic response.

> Dark blue, the mystic voyager,
>   gazing over waters, flowing wide.
> Where will he sail this day
>   searching for tomorrow's gold?
> Does he search the seas "in tune"
>   or seek a "fiddle" of his own?
> Is he bound to craft and sail
>   by illusion of his need?
> Or like us, by illusion of his greed?

The leaf and Dragonfly were gone, sped headlong on their journey by a swift rush of water.

An atmosphere of tranquility and peace settled over the river.

In the deep, dark hole upriver, within reach of the Weeping Willow fronds, a pair of Platypuses foraged early mornings and late evenings, but for the moment they too were at peace, quiet in their subterranean tunnel in the rich, protective earth. As if to defy the calm, a bold Rock Dragon scampered noisily across the dry-leaf carpet close by. The energy of Nature felt close, very close, an intensity contained in the calm.

It is interesting, I pondered, that Nature offers me no blueprint for cultural skill. I have my successes and failures in the garden, just as other people do. Strange, yet not really strange at all. To receive directed guidance would lead me into dependency, inadvertently creating and maintaining helplessness. I would not wish for that.

Such guidance from our kingdom would destroy your intuitive powers to attune with that center of "knowing."

The energy was new, a quality—or character—not previously experienced. "Knowing" put forward what I was seeking.

I glanced along the river bank to a young Mulberry tree not far from where I was sitting, perhaps the offspring from a bird-dropped fruit; it leaned over the water's edge, its large green leaves soaking up the energy of the sun.

"It is you I hear. Thank you for your words and for the rare occasions I can beat the birds to your fruit, thank you. I have tasted your delicacy both sides of the world."

The flow of words again slid smoothly into my awareness, and as often happens my line of thought was ignored.

Knowing is held in this moment—"now."

Prior thinking does not contain "knowing," while logic and reason deny the principle of "knowing." Reacting from fear, "knowing" is denied. Acting from love, "knowing" is.

The river swirled and rippled around the firm out-thrust bridge board on which I was sitting. I stripped off my clothes, folded my towel, and laid it along the diving end of the board.

Lying down, the sun warm on my back, I gazed into the water, staring straight down into the depths. A small Damselfly, slender and graceful, settled on a blade of Tussock Grass overhanging the water. In one smooth movement the long, slender abdomen arched, its tail end entering the surface of the river. Although it defied my eyesight, I knew that eggs were being pumped from its ovipositor into the water, there to attach themselves until the time of hatching. In moments the Damselfly was gone, but I could see the occasional, large Dragonfly, with down-curved abdomen, depositing eggs beneath the water surface in a series of long, skimming flights over the river.

The miracle of birth . . . and rebirth?

In the springtime when a larva hatches from its eggcase, a predator is born into the dense world of water. Voracious, ever hungry, the Dragonfly larva is deadly to all its size, a tiger of the deep. Much larger tadpoles perish, sucked empty by this killer larva. In the course of time, the natural cycle completed, the larva clambers up onto a rock or log into the light atmosphere of air. A metamorphosis takes place. There comes a moment when the casing of the larva splits and a Dragonfly emerges triumphant in the sunlight. A pause ... a few hours to pump powerful body enzymes through the wings, time to dry, firm, and strengthen ... and a new creature takes to the air. Did the larva in its dense water world know of the birthing to come, into the fine world of air? Did the Dragonfly have any memory of dying to a water world while birthing into an air world?

The metaphor hung over the river, dazzling in its obvious implication. Do we know from where we are born?

Maybe we are born into a dense world, a savage predator terrorizing and destroying life around us. In the course of time, the cycle complete upon our unconscious choice, we die to the dense world.

Is this our metamorphosis?

Are we reborn into the pure light of Spirit? Do we take wing, soaring on the high energy of controlled thought, free to take a higher nourishment, free to bask in the sunlight of that which "IS"?

Do we choose, in our desire for perfection, to once again enter the dense world, maybe for a quick splash, or perhaps a long swim, to attempt to redress the desire and fear which permeate the dense atmosphere, polluting our thoughts and actions? Could we be universal Dragonflies, immersed in a cosmic game in a Self-made world, seeking the cleansing and purification that only experience can offer?

6
March

I AM FREQUENTLY DRAWN to the river by an intensity, an insistent urge which demands.

The sun shines ... the river calls ... and I obey.

One morning, following such an intense urge, I was sitting on the diving board, poised over the vibrant and sparkling water, when I put forward the question:

"What is it that responds?"

Do not look for separation.

The I that calls is not separate from the I which responds.

To those who are aware of their sensitivity and are determined to cultivate and encourage their finer feelings, life calls in many varied ways.

For you, the river calls.

The river becomes a matrix.

The known falls back into its crucible. It is reborn, "knowing."

In the womb of Nature, water is the receptor of life ... and the birth giver.

"Do I answer a call from life that I may receive new birth?"

By choice you move with life as it "IS."

The clouded stream of human belief would drag you into its current of illusion, while the clear flow of Nature seeks to nurture the birthing of an ancient Self.

Two movements compete for attention. You must balance
these energies to emerge unscathed.

"Why do I feel such intensity? How is it that beneath my
calm approach to life a raging, seething discontent mingles easily with a serene acceptance?"

Your discontent is a blessing — give thanks for it.
Know where it is centered.
You are discontent with life's illusion. An inner "knowing"
rages against "known's" offerings.
The battlefield is a natural dynamic, a potent force to be
harnessed and directed, yet only through the power of surrender
to that which "IS." This is your training, your destiny.

"There is a destiny?"

If you so wish you can choose the when. Destiny was
accepted with awareness, but chosen before awareness knew of
choice.

I could feel concepts and ideas quite new to me shifting and
sifting as though we all floated interlocked in a deep, dark pool.
My sense of Self expanded, and, with the expansion, a focus
clarified.

The sensation was quite unlike telescopic vision, seeing
more of less and less. Instead, seeing with my eyes continued as
before, but I was not aware of looking through my eyes. I iden-
tified with all, seeing not "onto" with focus, but "identifying"
with an inner clarity.

I was the I which I observed.

The experience was strange, both new and familiar.

An orange-red Dragonfly settled on the diving board near
my journal. In seconds it was gone, yet in the going it remained.
The space was empty to normal vision, unoccupied by a
Dragonfly in a physical sense, yet a psychical knowing of
Dragonfly was as clear and focused as ever.

A sense of bewilderment swept over me; my brain was baffled by the speed of change.

I closed my eyes and relaxed. Vision was gone, but perception roamed like a child, blinking nervously in a new light. Was it visual impression, imagination, or real?

Subtle beyond subtlety, delicate beyond delicacy.

Momentarily I perceived as that which "IS." It was a moment of infinite tenderness.

"Why," I pleaded, "can I not maintain this?"

That which emerges from a matrix must grow. Would you deny this principle? Can you deny sound to hear Silence? Does birth precede death, or death precede birth, or are birth and death a misconception of that which "IS"?

"Are you deliberately working me, stretching me?"

I heard nothing, but the power of suggestion from a clear, inviting physical river which flooded over me was so strong that my next move needs no recording. Even before I hit the water, a cry was torn from my heart.

"Let me see that which I hear, please, let it be so."

I dived deep, and holding my breath I swam further than I had any right to swim on one lungful of air. I emerged not breathless, but with a sense of awe.

What happened under there?

To my physical senses water had engulfed me, and while swimming I was acutely aware of the river ... yet, on some other plane of experience, I swam in space. Around me was a vast emptiness, not sky blue or star filled, but sheer nothingness. Nothingness lasted for an eternity of swimming nowhere. A wave of desperation, of panic-tinged despair swept over me ... and I saw a nearby star.

Beyond it, around it, other stars swung lazily into position on smooth, silent orbits. Relief poured through me, and I swam toward them, torn between directions and wondering which was the nearest star.

Do not seek sanctuary in its cellular form, for that which I AM is the "nothing" of space. I swim in the universe of your Being.

You swim in the universe of that which "IS."

Look not for form, but from within see that which ener-
gizes form.

Hear not the sound, but the Silence which surrounds it. See
not the form, but the space of which it is formed.

While I swam in space, I swam unbreathing in the river, far
beyond one breath. It was a denial of time.

In space there is no time — real time.
In time there is no space — real space.
Can you unscramble this and taste truth?

Knowing was instantaneous. Realization came crashing in,
pounding through my head in a surging rush of blood.

For micro-moments the whole world stopped and all that
"IS" took an inbreath of pure newness. I was that newness.

For a cosmic Dragonfly the sun shone on gossamer wings
as the enzymes of a higher truth were catalyzed.

I dived again . . . greedily . . . but it was only a river in which
I swam.

A SUBTLE CHANGE was taking place in my relationship
with Nature. No longer was I on the outside looking in,
for the experience was developing in such a way that I
became the experience — experiencing.

For years I had listened to Nature's words while denying
them a place in reality; if everyone else was deaf then it was
easier for me to be deaf also. But now, in my surrender to an
inner truth, I found this strange reality demanding ever more of
me. And I mean demanding!

It was a turbulent day, the sun withdrawn and morose
behind the heavy clouds moving slowly across the sky. Wind
blew in fits and starts, gusting with huge energy for a few
moments, then subsiding with a mellow sigh.

The river called.

I sat in the living room, comfortable, trying to deny the call.

Why not listen to Nature's wisdom in comfort? Why the river, it's only a place? . . . and the river called.

With a sigh, I left the armchair, gathered my journal, and headed for the river. Passing under the Morton Bay Fig, I noticed some fresh cow dung covered with bright-green flies, shiny and immaculate in buzzing swarms. I had not previously noticed these flies.

Must be some autumn flies making a late appearance – to make a brief flight and mate before winter doth them part, I thought whimsically.

Using the hand rail with considerable care, I slowly descended the steep track down the bush-covered incline leading to my river refuge. Half an hour earlier it had been pouring rain, and the track was mud-slick slipperiness. Halfway down, one foot shot out from under me. Incredible! After twenty-five years I did a perfect breakfall, just as I had been trained in Judo classes in my late teens. I completed the journey with one very muddy forearm, but otherwise little the worse for wear.

"It had better be worth it," I growled . . . very quietly!

The river flowed, impassive as ever. In this moment, no place could look less inviting, or less mystical. Mundane was the word I was feeling for this place and mood. I sat on the diving board and, on cue, the wind came gushing down the river, snatching at my journal and playing indifferently with the leaping pages. The sun, pale and watery, peered from behind the lacy masking of a gray cloud. Around me, high in the branches of the trees, my friend the wind sang her unique song of creation as she whipped the leaves to a frenzy.

Would you deny the wind while accepting the river?

Hurling a violent gust into the branches above my head, the wind held me in comparative calm. "I am as prepared to accept you as conscious energy as I am any other aspect of Nature," I responded.

I feel you are truthful.

Was it coincidence? The wind fell away to the softest gentle murmur.

In the Oneness from which I spring I am aware of your attunement with Nature. I am involved in every moment of your experience. I am wind, composed of air—a basic element.
For you I am life.
For this world I am life.
For beyond, I exist in a nonexistent state.

There was a pause. I had nothing to offer. Startling in its sudden power, an immense gust of wind shook the trees around me. Feeling a touch of humor I mumbled—"Tut tut."

The wind was gone, the trees empty of movement. A strange awareness grew slowly around me. I was wrong. Things were not what they seemed. The leaves above me continued to sway and dance, singing the high song of the wind . . . yet there was Silence, the wind static in my Being.

A duality of experience emerged. There was wind—and no wind. There was sound—and Silence. Movement—and stillness.

Each action offered its moment of truth to my physical and psychical Selves.

I knew my challenge was to synthesize the movements, denying neither experience. To move with both, accepting as "IS."

Joy and tenderness leapt to the surface of my awareness. I gazed with inner, loving eyes at two aspects of Self, comfortable and aware in their togetherness. For several moments an awareness of "IS" held a trinity of identity . . . then the sun emerged, flooding illumination over all experience.

I became the I who relates to everyday life. I became the I knowing who I am. I became the I which "IS."

Just as I tear the feeble hold of exhausted leaves from a tree, so will I tear old, spent concepts from your feeble grasp. Your path is one of surrender. To release, let go. This requires courage in human terms. The path of unknowing, knowing, knowing "IS."

I smiled at the absurdity of an inadequate language.

Well you may smile, but Nature can only express through "you" in your language.

While we have the capacity to expand, destroy, replace, and revitalize your concepts of life, you are the controller of your words.

"Would you like me to learn new words to expand my vocabulary?"

Only as a natural organic movement. As you flow and expand, so will your ability to fully express yourself develop with you.

We have stated before — we desire openness and simplicity. Your gift is communication through simplicity. Do not destroy it.

"I guess you are referring to the human me I know. Being smart holds little appeal."

You are smart enough. To attune with Nature requires neither smartness nor cleverness.

One requires humility. Humility to recognize your inherent "greatness," and a humility which recognizes the "greatness" as a part of the universal "IS."

Remember, my friend, as you fly the sun spaces in your unfolding experiencing of nothing, remember wind and its substance — nothing; no-thing.

The words echoed with mystery. We humans are mystery, surrounded by mystery. What an empty mockery to live life only in the pursuit of money and pleasure if it requires we sacrifice the mystery of what "IS."

On Tracy's coffee mug are the words: "Life is not a problem to be solved, but a mystery to be lived."

In this moment the mystery was paramount, vibrating in wind and life with intense energy. Maybe the way of life is to continually inquire, seeking no answers, yet this is not easy to accomplish for we are then involved in the concepts of "letting go" and "being." Vague words and meanings, but I suspect that our destiny is to give these concepts meaning and purpose.

To inquire suggests that we seek always to explore rather than exploit—to seek, rather than find—to live life as an open-ended agreement with God, rather than search for a nonexistent conclusion. How can that which has no ending be concluded?

T HE DAY WAS CALM but cloudy. This time the river was not calling; instead, I felt a desire to commune with the river.

When I approached the water, it lacked the sparkle of dancing reflections which only the sun can produce. There was a calm, an expectancy the river was very alive.

A bottle bobbing high in the water floated toward me from upriver. It moved swiftly under the Willow tree and headed with speed and purpose toward the old bridge board on which I was sitting.

As it slowly floated over the deep pool where the Platypuses hunt, the bottle was suddenly out of the mainstream, surging in hapless circles around and around in a slow, eddying swirl.

There was a flow to the river, but the bottle no longer rode with it. How many human bottles do I know?

For how long did I helplessly circle, a human out of the flow of life?

Questions sprang to my mind as I watched the almost-stationary bottle, but answers were not required. The sense of purpose which motivates us feeds us an illusion of being in life's mainstream; yet, in truth, we are in life's river, slowly eddying in a backwater, while the surging current of activity passes by. We have a divine right to life which we can never lose, but to be in life's flow instead of a backwater is a choice we have to make and direct.

All humanity is contained in the river of life, but the slow, deep holes and the fast, shallow rapids offer their deception.

When you are aware and awake you may correctly interpret them; if you do not, then you are at their mercy.

A movement in the water below caught my attention. In the calm, clear water a Leopard Eel moved with purposeful grace along the rock ledges on the riverbed. Its whole intent was obvious—a hunting forage. Sinuous and calm, the Eel sought its prey, poking in each hole and crevice with deadly efficiency. He was not very big, a shade under one yard perhaps. Some of our Leopard Eels can reach almost two yards, with a large girth and dappling along their backs. They are the rulers of the underwater world in our stretch of the river. A flurry, and a half-grown Catfish shot out of a crevice. The Eel ignored it, continuing its slow, careful inspection with alert intensity. It probably had shrimps on the menu!

The Eel has a sense of purpose, and hunger is the motivation, but be aware of how little of the river each Eel patrols.

I knew of their territorial habits, each staking a claim on their choice of the riverbed. In some areas, while lying half hidden alongside submerged logs, the larger and therefore unmolested Eels (they are less competitive and nervous) have let me gently stroke along their soft bellies, my fingers caressingly persuading them to half roll onto their sides. Over a summer period, I have established a genuine rapport with certain Eel characters.

It is not the purpose of mankind to stake a claim and stay forever fixed. Only fear needs to hold onto an area, naming it "home," a place of safety. There are those, however, for whom this meets their needs and their purpose, for in establishing roots they make real growth.

But man is not a tree.

Greater growth is experienced when roots are kept trimmed, never seizing hold of an area to make it "mine."

Let ownership begin when it is no longer needed. While security demands ownership, then it is stagnation in the guise of comfort which will bind you.

The river flows — on, ever on.

Let home be a base, but never a purpose, or like the Eel, your limitations will control you.

When you look into the water do you see last week's water, or yesterday's . . . or is the water ever fresh, ever flowing, ever new?

I am almost ashamed to record it, but my eyes, from their conditioned limits, had never seen the river as totally "new." I saw the same river, the same water. My eyes lied to me, while my mind fostered the lie. The water is new, it is continuous newness, and although intellectually I knew this, my eyes had never transcended their conditioning.

Yet I had "felt" the newness of water.

I had been aware of the aliveness of water; only my eyes were deceived.

Now . . . I looked at the river anew.

What did I expect? Did I assume it would look different? It did not. It looked like the river usually looks. Again . . . I was the difference. I realized that the difference will never lie in the observed, only in the observer.

As I scrambled back up the steep track, I was speculating on "fresh" water. Fresh as in new! I walked into the kitchen, and, as it was lunch time, I accepted an offer of poached eggs on toast. While I watched Treenie preparing my meal, I realized that the "fresh"-water principle applied to people as well. When I wake up in the morning, do I see yesterday's Treenie, again with deceived eyes, or can I see a new Treenie by seeing "anew"? If I see a new Treenie, and she sees a new Michael, our relationship will be fresh, new, vital, and alive. If, however, we see yesterday's partner, then we each become the cause of stagnation and repetition in our relationship.

Always you are each the causative factor.

Today's people seen through yesterday's eyes will swing you out of the mainstream of the river of life into an eddying swirl of stagnation.

For some unfortunate people this is called marriage. See

*your partner in life, all people, as totally "new" in the moment
of contact.*

*In this way you may live confined to one area, yet flowing
swiftly in the fresh current of life.*

*Life will seek you, rather than you being the seeker of life.
Thus the paradox is revealed. To live life constantly on the
move, yet viewing through "yesterday's" eyes, denies movement or change.*

*To live life from one home, on one tiny plot of land, viewing
all life through "today's" eyes, allows you to be the aperture
through which life flows, ever fresh, ever new.*

*However, for those who roam far and wide, ever moving,
ever aware, ever open, viewing all life through "this moment's"
eyes ... life becomes a benediction.*

I was quiet, humbled by the magnitude of life and growth
which yet awaits me.

THERE WAS A TIME when the valley in which I live contained an abundant flood of forest pouring from the
plateau escarpment down into the valley. Among its
trees the Red Cedar (*Toona australis*) was a giant, a king among
trees, and the only deciduous tree in the forest. That time has
passed. In his folly, man plundered the valuable harvest of
timber, leaving the valley barren of its former richness. Only a
few Red Cedars survived, for this timber was the most valuable
and desired of all.

Sitting in our garden area under one such tree, I studied the
few Red Cedars dotted among the Citrus trees near our house.
Although tall to an uneducated eye, these trees were mere sap-
lings, no more than sixty feet high. Over the rough bark a mass
of epiphytic orchids crept their way from limb to limb, slowly smothering each branch with a mat of thick, fleshy leaves.
Jammed in the forks of larger branches, huge Orchids were
clumped in thickets, offering their flowers each season as a

blessed compensation. Dotted throughout each tree, hanging from the limbs with casual indifference to location, the fronds of Elkhorn and Staghorn Ferns were seen among the foliage.

It was early autumn, but the Cedars remained green. Many weeks were needed before a winter chill denied the flow of sap to dependent leaves.

I am not a botanist and I know little of the age of tree species, but I feel the energy of Red Cedars as very old. A wisdom of some long-forgotten order is fostered by these trees, but it is not of a physical nature. Its roots go beyond the physical outreach of a tree. A gray sky framed another overcast day and invoked a brooding atmosphere, yet the energy seemed focused on the aura of a forgotten glory in some past era. In some strange way I felt my awareness drawn into a past, floating as though on a cloud of light above the brooding intensity up onto, or into, a dimension of inner visual impression.

From an inner seeing, soaring high above the valley, I gazed onto immense stands of forest in some timeless zone.

What I perceived bordered on fantasy, for it was "feeling" vision, rather than "seeing" vision. No doubt my eyes would protest if shown a forest of long ago, growing rich and abundant with towering Red Cedars on farmland which is now smooth and green with Kikuyu-dominated pasture.

Perception suggested that my eyes did not contain all truth, merely one level of truth to which we totally relate. Today's movies make mockery of the old saying—"Seeing is believing." Our eyes are limited, feeding us deceit and falsity along with correct impression. Perception also suggested that my experience of life would be richer if I opened myself to multiple levels of experience, rather than only a visual and auditory experience confined to three-dimensional planes.

With Silence came clarity.

The time when great forests filled many valleys such as this, is not separate from this time.
In the dimension to which mankind relates, the forests

have disappeared, while those remaining are threatened with destruction. A moment in passing.

This is the reality with which man is in accord, but it is not reality as "IS."

If life did not supply the exact Law of Cause and Effect to your sense of reality, you could learn nothing. Learning requires that you experience the polarity of action. Yet mankind is not confined to physical reality.

Man may realize his greater awareness, probing into higher zones of truth and reality.

Fly high over the forests and feed your heart, for the forests are more real than the illusion which denies them a physical counterpart.

For an alarming moment, a reasoning mind protested to an illumined spirit at the strangeness of the dual experience, but it subsided. As far as the inner "I" could see, a rich carpet of luxurious forest covered the valley, while a sparkling river of crystal water wandered with serpentine grace under the canopy of trees.

While I, the infinite soul Self, gazed from above, I, the finite physical Self, sat in a chair, journal on my lap, quiet and at peace with my surroundings. My acceptance of the experience felt good. To smoothly synthesize the experiencing of two Selves, each a contradiction to the sense receptors of the other mode of experience, was less of an achievement than a surrender.

In surrendering protest, denial, and doubt, you lose nothing, but gain insight and courage.

In surrendering Self to an ongoing process, that which is lost is the "known," while that which is "knowing" is gained — but cannot be known.

"Knowing" is realized knowledge.

The moment when the "known" ignites, leaving only the ash of truth, is a spontaneous "knowing."

The gathering of energy faded, and sadly my limited normality returned. The physical world became my focal point, casting me back once more into the illusion of isolation. The Red Cedars around me were, to all intents and purposes, just trees, growing in our world, yet remote from us, separate and unconnected.

I believe that our welfare as nations of peoples lies with the development of the ability to truly see our place in the scheme of life. So long as we are separated and remote from Nature, we are isolated from a deeper relationship with each other, and unable to trust and accept the "one" race of humanity.

MARCH WAS CLOSING ANOTHER CHAPTER when I walked with care and caution down to "my place" by the river. The day seemed to carry an intensity, and the river was so alive when I sat on the diving board over the water, that just being with it as an observer required my full attention. In the depths below, a solitary Golden Perch swam in slow, lazy circles. It was a newcomer, and I admired the faint gold tinge outlining each scale. This was a bold fish, obviously quite unthreatened as it stared up at me from swiveled eyes. Two ducks flew from upriver, literally running along the water surface for a short distance before gaining flight. A yellow butterfly fluttered past, falling and rising in erratic flight.

Mullet and Herring leaped from the water, while Fantails and Blue Wrens flitted, chattering and scolding, among the branches above my head. A special day, quite superb.

You do not see the perfection in every day, in every moment?

I was vaguely surprised at the question. I had been enrapt in my observations and feelings. Although I was open to the river's subtle energy, it caught me unexpectedly.

The question also hurt. In honesty—no—I did not see and feel the perfection in every moment, in every day. I would like to, but the simple fact is: my environment has a huge influence on me.

When each moment is born anew in your consciousness, you will carry no more pain. In rebirth, the newborn may choose perfection.

Again, surprise flickered through me. The reference to pain was very meaningful. During our years in Tasmania I had injured my back, and incompetent medical attention had allowed a chronic condition to develop. With hindsight I acknowledge that the pain had been a great catalyst in my life, but to this day it pursued me, blending months of freedom with times of intense suffering. Having just emerged from a week of back pain and limitation, I would give a lot to be free of it.

You have only to release the desire to suffer.

Anger suddenly swept over me. To suggest I desired suffering was ridiculous. Unexpectedly, the river physically intervened. In the water below, a Water Tortoise walked with dignified speed along the riverbed. Its long snakelike neck and head were well extended, while it traveled in an easy floating glide. This graceful movement from such an inherently clumsy creature contrasted greatly with the ungainly crawl of a Land Tortoise. I am not sure whether the Australian Tortoise took to the water, or never left it, but it was a smart move. None are land bound.

The Land Tortoise carries its heavy load, making slow progress.
Gravity is the pressure.
In the river the Tortoise is relieved of its weight. Gravity is no longer a pressure. It is not atmospheric gravity which limits mankind, but the gravity of limited thinking, of bound, restricted thought.
If you were to place all your grave burdens into the river of life, allowing the "IS" to carry you, the freedom you would experience could not manifest as back pain.
Only the weight of an overload manifests as back pain.
Unconscious — subconscious — conscious, the load is car-

ried on mental levels beyond the physical capacity. This over-load manifests in disease, sickness, injury, and pain.

The words were clear, and for a long time I have intellectually known their meaning. But how? How do we just let go?

Such a move requires a major surrender. A surrender of the ego with all its little "i"s fighting for survival.

It really is not difficult. You need accept only one truth—and live it.

THIS MOMENT IS PERFECT. Know it. Become it. Live it. Breathe it. Stay with it. Become centered on it.

Perfection will move from an uncomfortable, painful, demanding, unpleasant, limited perfection . . . to a perfection of freedom, peace, acceptance, expansion, limitlessness.

Life will move from rigidity to fluidity.

Pain is a symptom. Rigidity is a cause.

To break rigidity may cause pain; to retain it "is" pain.

Rigidity resists, fluidity resists not—nor does it pain.

Fluidity is not what you do, but how you do it.

Fluidity or rigidity is the state of mind in action. Treating sickness may repair effect, but it does not touch cause. At best it may be the catalyst which allows cause to be recognized and changed.

The freedom of fluidity is found by knowing that whatever you desire you already have.

For you—your body is saying, "Release suffering, allow me to be healed," while you are saying, "No, I need the pain lest I forget I am not free."

Release it. You are free. Know it.

My head was beginning to spin. I took a deep breath . . . slowing down. . . . Silence. . . . An inner dialogue moved through me with gentle freedom. I was unattached to thought or meaning. It is possible. I can be free of pain. I no longer need pain when I can accept freedom. But . . . I cannot accept freedom because I have just realized . . . I do not recognize it. I don't know freedom.

Clarity moved whisper-soft over the dialogue.

Freedom is "now." In no other time or space may it be real. Only "now". . . forever. I had known that also for a long time, but again . . . only in my head. An idea. A concept. Never real . . . because I had pain.

Maybe this is another new beginning. I feel movement as the knowing connects head and heart. It fits.

The Water Tortoise returned, drifting across the river bed in a slow, scrabbling glide. Nearing the rocks close to the diving board, it slowly surfaced, its head breaking the water into clean, small ripples. Mouth open, the Tortoise gulped in air.

Suddenly it saw me; our eyes met in a moment of contact . . . and it was gone in a hurried rush of water, plunging to the riverbed. I heard no words, but in the one penetrating glance I read a clear message.

"Which of us is encased in the toughest shell?"

As I stood up on the diving board, acute pain flared in my lower back causing me to stretch and ease the cramped muscles carefully.

I felt the weight of limits, of rigidity, as I stared into the empty depths.

"Which indeed?"

7
April

FROM AN EARLY AGE I have recognized a connection with Nature, a mystical thread moving beyond mind and heart, connecting me to some mysterious, unknown element. That I am not alone in this connection is proven by the mystical writings of the ages, yet for some reason mankind as a whole has failed to realize this inner truth.

The cities with their choked masses surely deny the space and time to find the Self which experiences further realities. I have been fortunate, surrounded in my early days by fields of golden corn; of meadows green; by the woods of Oak, Beech, Sycamore, Elm, and other friends; by cold rivers and mystic ponds; and later as an adult by the splendor of Australia's coastal bush, by the damp and dripping rain forest, the highland lakes, the crystal rivers which man has not yet poisoned, and mountains which gaze blindly to the stars. These have always been within easy reach. Our previous home was in an environment of Nature's extravagance unleashed. Its location in a valley not far from where we now live was idyllic. The land encompassed rain forest, hills, and tiny valleys in a setting of outstanding beauty. A river snaked its way along the base of the forest-covered escarpment, forming one of our natural boundaries. A few hundred yards along the river a dense thicket of Bamboo thrived and expanded, growing larger with each passing season.

The Bamboo became my hideaway sanctuary. It was a place to indulge my self-pity, or to shrug away the pain of a wounded ego. A place of quiet. A tiny, hidden track twisted through the Bamboo to a certain log lying full length in the river. Pointing downstream, the log offered no resistance to flood waters, and it had lain on the river bed for a long time. This was Lizard Lounge, the ultimate sunbathing skinny-dipping hideaway.

Log, river, and Bamboo combined to form a place of synthesis, a matrix of holistic energy. Even after we left our previous home I would often make return visits, and after chatting for a while I would head off to Lizard Lounge and the Bamboo grove.

One such day at noon, I walked down to the Bamboo to consciously reconnect with the energies of Nature I had experienced there in my earlier days of doubt and conflict. Creeping into the center of the grove I sat down, journal on my lap. The magic was as strong as ever.

Sunlight danced a slow, rhythmic pattern over the deep litter of fallen leaves on which I sat. Cool and mysterious, the Bamboo invoked memories of pain and joy, no longer separate, but blended by time. Below me, the same river to which I attune where we now live sighed quietly as it flowed around the bulk of Lizard Lounge. Whipbirds called forth their rolling, delayed whip . . . crack, exploding the quiet of the Bamboo grove.

Earth breathed out a pungent, rich organic aroma, while Silence settled like an invisible mist. Surrounding me, the green, smooth barrels of Bamboo stems rose slender toward the blue sky, rising twelve feet before the first thin branchlets of foliage sprang from the splendid pillars of supple strength. Tenderly adding movement to the magic, a breeze stole quietly through the pale-green leaves above my head, causing shadows and sunspots to flicker and dance in soundless motion. Peace . . . a peace beyond words embraced me, holding me safe for a few timeless, precious moments.

Your presence is welcome. You are reconnecting with an awareness which is likened to weak eyes blinking before the

*sun. Yet, unlike your eyes, awareness can endure the blazing
light, growing stronger, expanding, opening to ever-wider vistas.*

*You have walked often in our midst, blind to our subtlety,
deaf to our whispers of truth. Now you return, with the birth of
wholeness nurturing in your heart.*

We welcome you as a human, as humanity.

*Man is of one kind, of one energy. In our midst all human-
ity is contained in your holistic Being.*

The peace intensified, becoming a movement within, disturbing deep long-forgotten emotions. I became aware of a Oneness of joy and grief. My normal senses have shown me that joy
and grief are separate, each expressing very different emotions
and reactions; in these experiences, joy and grief are one. Joy contains grief, and grief only fulfills and expands joy. Often I weep
from pain of the limited Self, yet the weeping is a confused reaction to a transcendent joy tinged with pain. I do not understand
these emotions. I do not know their origin. I cannot identify
them. I only know my experience of higher realities has shown
me that without pain, joy becomes shallow. Without the "falling
to earth" there can be no "transcendent flight."

The inner movement of peace became a gentle, poignant
vibration. One could say I felt a subtle inner shift, a moment of
separation, and again the duality of experience began.

Shadows and sun splashes flickered around me, dancing
fragments of light playing over body and Bamboo. I felt a confusion, for it seemed the Bamboos were fragmenting and disinte-
grating around me, while my own body was caught in this magi-
cal dance of light. As though lifted by a wind of some inner
source, I was blown out of the Bamboo thicket and into a universe of color-filled sound and sound-filled color.

No longer was I fragmented. A single being, united, I
watched from billions of inner "I"s as I became at "One" with
the human song of pain . . . and joy.

Become centered on that which "IS."

There is an immense pressure in the human mind to

believe in a tiny truth. Embrace it ... own it ... but do not deny
a vast truth ... your truth ... human truth.

Listen to the collective human song, but do not be afraid
to sing your own song. Dance to the music which moves in your
Being. Follow the star in your heart until perfectly positioned in
all that "IS."

Be a player in the game of life, but be aware of the golden
rule ... the player controls the moves ... the player is the mover
... the player is the moved.

My inner view of life changed as it expanded. I have no
words to describe visible sound forming intangible networks of
space, or ways to explain ideas of pure energy framing new
worlds.

Holistic experiencing peaked ... timeless ... until, caught
in a giant wind, I was blown as a leaf in a storm ... of peace ...
my field of experiencing narrowing ... until I gazed once more
on dancing splashes of light playing over pale-green Bamboo
stems.

Momentarily I felt shaky. The subtlety of the experience
was overwhelming. Self-doubt could so easily destroy it. When I
arose, it was to scramble down the track to Lizard Lounge, only
available by a swim in the cold, autumn water. My introspective
mood denied the swim as I stood caught in deep thought.
Whenever I experience this "exaltation," a paradox is always
revealed. I had simultaneously experienced separation and connection. I was filled with a knowing that fragmentation and
wholeness are inseparable.

Separation and connection, fragmentation and wholeness —
all are strands in a single universal thread. While all threads are
woven into the human experience as one energy, it is we who
separate the strands.

Separation is a concept. One in which we believe. A concept
which has become the law of the land. But believing a misconception does not change truth. Truth — all life ... connected ...
"IS."

DAY AFTER DAY A STEADY RAIN had been falling, and just as steadily the river crept higher and higher. On the fourth morning I slithered down the slope through the dripping bush to our water pump, switching off the electric motor to prevent later problems. Below me the water surged quietly without the violence that torrential rain produces. Moving with as much stealth as I could muster, I crept through the drenched undergrowth, finally emerging at my special place.

The river was high, lapping just beneath our diving board. With much difficulty, I dragged the heavy old bridge board higher into the safety of the bush. This place I love so much, of wild bush and rocks, is a bend in the river; thus, even when the river is subdued, the water laps both sides of the jutting outcrop, creating a feeling of island.

Standing in the rain, the swollen river seemed to almost split at my feet, moving into the blind-inlet side with turbulent energy, while flowing with smooth, hurrying power downriver.

As I gazed into the rain upstream, I appeared to stand in the center of the river, the water hastening to my inner call. For a long time I stood there, feeling the river as a whole entity, knowing it from an inner level as a source of joy and inspiration. No longer was the water flowing around me, for my awareness expanded wider and wider, embracing and drawing the river through the center of my Being. With the river came overwhelming joy and gratitude. I called aloud into the rain.

"Thank you for all you have given me, for all you have shown me. You have extended an honor I will not abuse."

The joy swelled, tears mingled with the rain on my cheeks.

We have given you nothing.
We have shown you nothing.
It is you who have learned how to accept the fruit which is always on offer to mankind. The fruit of human wisdom will fall delicately into the hand when one reaches out in love and humility. This fruit cannot be plucked from the tree of life, nor can it be plundered at the roots.

It is you who have looked into the waters and have seen the reflected truth. When the eyes of mankind are blinded by fear, only desire and greed may be reflected. You have used the clarity of Nature to perceive the clarity residing in the human heart.

The richness of a holistic life is the sponsor of your joy, the promoter of your tears.

I stood silently, utterly absorbed in a real world where Nature's movement is of total order. Out on the river a small, black object caught my attention, bringing my focus back to a normal sense reality. I had often wondered how the Platypus fared in times of flood; now I knew.

Like a leaf in a playful breeze, the Platypus flowed and rippled with the swirling water—one moment floating with short legs and webbed feet extended, bright eyes surveying overhead happenings, the next beneath the murky surface while feeding on the rich harvest offered by the flood waters.

Here was no battle with the current, no fight to prove its mastery. The Platypus took the power and energy of the river and used it. As an Eagle masters the wild thermals of upper air, so the Platypus rode the currents of swirling water. I extended myself to that innocent master, reading its intent as it plunged deep into the water. As One we submerged, all direction and senses lost in the whirling confusion of river and debris.

The Platypus foraged and surveyed, moving in scrabbling, supple, clumsy grace, a master of its environment.

Abruptly I lost contact, standing alone and dripping on the rocks, vaguely wondering if it had ever been real. I stood and watched, pupil and teacher, while a solitary ancient creature, primitive and unique, taught me how to ride the currents of the river of life . . . effortlessly.

There came a moment in mid-river; the Platypus did not reappear.

Thus we disappear, each in our time, each in our own way, but, like the Platypus, we, too, will reemerge at a different time, a different place, to again swim in the river of life. One river only in which all life swims. One river, one life. One movement held in one moment. The river is not the mystery, only the swim.

I stood entranced, while rain dripping in huge drops from the foliage overhead soaked through my raincoat and into my clothes.

Somewhere the Platypus had reemerged, for while I saw nothing . . . I felt its presence as surely as the promise of a new tomorrow.

About the Author

Michael J. Roads was born in Trumpington, Cambridge, England in 1937. In 1964 he emigrated to Tasmania, Australia where for the next twelve years he followed a career in beef and dairy farming. During this period Michael left behind conventional farming methods and switched to organic farming. This move encompassed a dramatic inner change which allowed him to reconnect with nature.

In 1976, after selling their farm, Michael and Treenie Roads and their four children spent nearly a year traveling throughout Australia. In 1977 he initiated the Homeland Foundation Community in Bellingen Valley which is modeled on Findhorn.

His first book, *A Guide to Organic Gardening in Australia*, was the first book written on this subject in Australia and was published in 1976. His second book, *A Guide to Organic Living in Australia*, was published in 1977. Both these books were Australian best sellers.

In addition to writing full time, Michael is a workshop leader. He gives talks on the Spirit of Nature and with Treenie teaches a seminar "On Being Free."

Books that Transform Lives

The Earth Life Series
By Sanaya Roman, Channel for Orin

Living with Joy, *Book I*
"I like this book because it describes the way I feel about so many things." — Virginia Satir

Personal Power through Awareness, *Book II*
"Every sentence contains a pearl...." Lilias Folan

Way of the Peaceful Warrior
By Dan Millman

"It may even change the lives of many...who peruse its pages." — Dr. Stanley Krippner

Opening to Channel: How to Connect with Your Guide
by Sanaya Roman and Duane Packer, Ph.D.

This breakthrough book is the first step-by-step guide to the art of channeling!

Seeds of Light
By Peter Rengel

"Simple is powerful." — Dan Millman

H J Kramer Inc
America's Fastest Growing New Age Spiritual Publisher